Enjoy the book!

Bill Rutherford

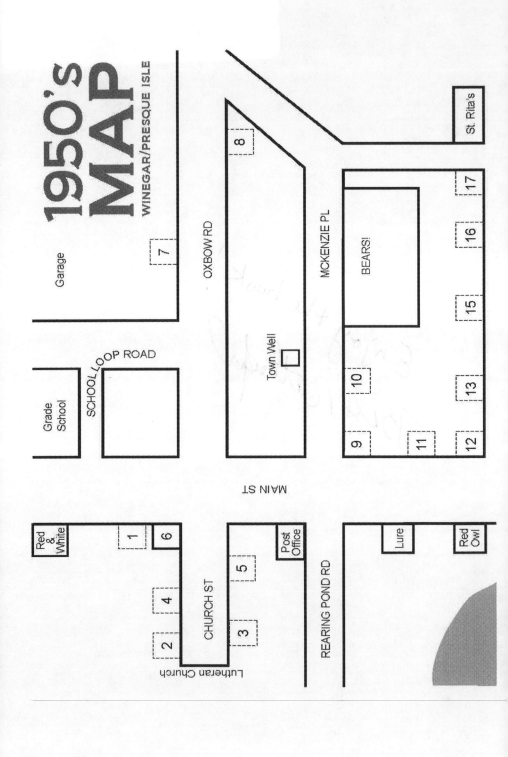

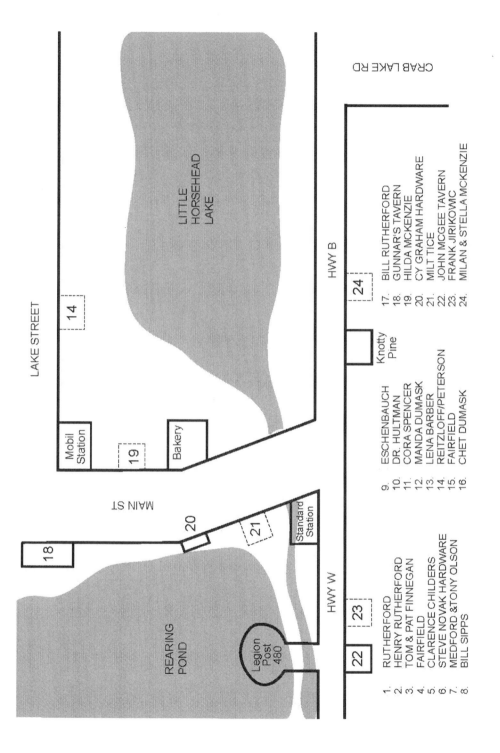

LAKE STREET

LITTLE
HORSEHEAD
LAKE

14

19

Mobil
Station

Bakery

MAIN ST

18

20

21

Standard
Station

REARING
POND

Legion
Post
480

HWY W

22

23

HWY B

24

Knotty
Pine

CRAB LAKE RD

1. RUTHERFORD
2. HENRY RUTHERFORD
3. TOM & PAT FINNEGAN
4. FAIRFIELD
5. CLARENCE CHILDERS
6. STEVE NOVAK HARDWARE
7. MEDFORD &TONY OLSON
8. BILL SIPPS

9. ESCHENBAUCH
10. DR. HULTMAN
11. CORA SPENCER
12. MANDA DUMASK
13. LENA BARBER
14. REITZLOFF/PETERSON
15. FAIRFIELD
16. CHET DUMASK

17. BILL RUTHERFORD
18. GUNNAR'S TAVERN
19. HILDA MCKENZIE
20. CY GRAHAM HARDWARE
21. MILT TICE
22. JOHN MCGEE TAVERN
23. FRANK JIRIKOWC
24. MILAN & STELLA MCKENZIE

Winegar Reflections

Tales from
Wisconsin's North Woods

Winegar Reflections

Tales from
Wisconsin's North Woods

BILL RUTHERFORD

Wasteland Press

www.wastelandpress.net
Shelbyville, KY USA

Winegar Reflections:
Tales from Wisconsin's North Woods
by Bill Rutherford

First Printing – June 2016
ISBN: 978-1-68111-114-8
Cover by Nicole Heeti

Printed in the U.S.A.

0   1   2   3   4

To my dear grandchildren, Elia and Ezi Nichols:
It is my sincere wish that you both will enjoy reading this
book as much as I enjoyed writing it for you.

To Mr. Chet Dumask,
who was willing to share his incredible knowledge,
memories, and stories with me. Without his input this
book would not have been possible.
THANK YOU, CHET!

TABLE OF CONTENTS

Introduction..1

Life in the Outfield...3

"Timber-r-r-r-r-r-r!"..9

Winegar Massacre..17

Bullets and Bloodshed at Little Bohemia...........................24

Death Knell for a Small Town..31

Readin', Writin', and 'Rithmetic….....................................35

Higher Learning...46

Sunday Mass..48

The Great Paper Protest..56

Mouse in the House..61

A Visit from "Da Bears"..67

Hot Pursuit..73

"Uh, Dad… The House is on Fire!"...................................80

Fred Wolter Changes the Town...86

Don't Go Near the Water!...89

Fresh Bakery..95

Fun for all Seasons...97

Christmas Tree Hunting...102

A Boy and His Toys..110

It Was A Dark and Scary Night…......................................114

Northwoods Notables...124

Winegar Reflections...133

INTRODUCTION

It's amazing!

It's amazing how one question from a child can snowball into a year-long project and the fulfillment of a life-long ambition. But that is exactly how this book came to be.

"Grandpa, what was it like when you were a kid?" my granddaughter Elia implored. This innocent question prompted me to think about my childhood, and my years of growing up in Presque Isle, known as "Wisconsin's Last Wilderness", and I came to the realization that I had much to tell.

The following is the true story of growing up in a much simpler and safer time, a time before computers, cell phones, the internet and iPads. It is the story of life in a small town nestled in the north woods.

Presque Isle is, and was, usually a very quiet and peaceful little village. Well, except for the bears, murderers, moonshiners, gangsters, lumberjacks, and armed outlaws. Other than those minor details, it was always quite tranquil and, as you'll discover in the following pages, the perfect place for a boy to grow up.

Note: - the name of the town prior to 1955 was Winegar. Both names referenced in this book refer to the same town, just reflect different time periods. So, while it shows up on the map as "Presque Isle, to most of us it will always be "Winegar".

Since our book is all about life in a small American town, let's begin with a story involving that all-American sport- baseball....

Life in the Outfield

"Little League baseball is wonderful, because it keeps the kids out of the house...."

-Yogi Berra

The following is my recollection of the most memorable baseball game I was ever involved in while living in Presque Isle:

It's a warm and sunny Sunday at the end August and we are getting ready to play our final baseball game of the season. The town had gotten enough of us boys interested and last year we formed what could loosely be described as a "little league" team. Jack Long, owner of the Lure, was our coach, and the team had about 14 players. As one of the youngest players on the team, I didn't get to play much, but that may have been due more to my complete lack of athletic ability rather than my age. I probably would have been a good player except that I lacked the skills of hitting the ball and catching it. (About the only skill I did have was running, so I would have made a hall of fame pinch runner, but our team didn't use them back then, darn it!)

We played against other nearby towns, including Winchester, Boulder Junction, and Manitowish Waters; however, our biggest rival was the team from Marenisco, Michigan, a town some ten miles to our north - and the team we would be playing against today. I guess this would have been an early form of the "border wars" that take place when two teams from adjoining states compete with each other. Both of the teams were pretty good and we had beaten them by a slim margin at the beginning of June. They had, however, whipped us pretty soundly the next time we played, so this game was to be the all-important rubber game, which would decide who held bragging rights for the foreseeable future, or at least until basketball season started.

The games were played on the ball diamond next to the grade school, at the north end of town. A new backstop had been constructed in the spring, and the bleachers were usually full since this was a great way for families to spend a Sunday afternoon. This was true even when we played 'away' games, since the towns we played were fairly close by, and fans of both teams came to watch the action.

Because of my previously mentioned lack of baseball skills, I knew what position I would be occupying every game, which was the space at the far end of the bench. To be honest, I really didn't mind that so much, since I was just glad to be part of the team. And it is not like I didn't try to improve my almost non-existent abilities; I just never developed them into any level of acceptable play. During practice, I would certainly run after fly balls, and attempt diving stops of grounders hit in my direction, though these attempts were not usually successful. As poor as my fielding techniques were, they paled in comparison to my absolute failure at the plate. (I personally think the bat was too heavy, since by the time I had completed my swing at the ball, the catcher usually was already standing up and had thrown the ball halfway back to the pitcher).

We had some talented athletes on our team, mainly Bob Hill, Roger Peterson, and my two cousins, Tom and Pat Finnegan. The Hartmann boys- Jesse and Gary, were also pretty good, so we were able to stack up well against the larger towns in the area.

But back to today's game. It is now 1:00 o'clock and the contest gets underway. The first inning is scoreless but, in the top of the second, one of the Marenisco boys hits a two run homer to give them the lead. In the bottom of the third, we strike back as Roger Peterson hits a triple down the left field line that drives in Tom Finnegan and Gary Hartmann to tie the score. We take the lead in the fourth, when we are able to score two more runs due to some timely hits and great base running. The score is now 4-2 in our favor.

As the sixth, and final inning begins, with our lead still intact, I am shocked when I hear Mr. Long call my name. "Billy! Billy Rutherford! Go in left field!"

Me?? In the game?? Holy Cow!!! I grab my well-oiled, but seldom used glove, and rush out onto the field for only the second time all season. (the first time being a blow-out 12-4 win over the Boulder Junction team, during which time I mostly had to just stand there as our pitcher mowed down one batter after another). Apparently our coach felt we had the game well in hand, and had decided to give me a taste of playing in the final inning of the final game of the year. As you will discover, this almost proved to be a disastrous decision on his part, and one which could have gotten both him and I banned from further residence in the town.

There is one out, but two line drives down the right field line have brought the potential go-ahead run to the plate. There is a definite tension in the air, since the boy swinging the bat is one of Marenisco's biggest and best players. I, however, don't feel any of this tension since I am too excited just to be in the game. Instead of paying attention to the action, I am scanning the crowd, where I see my parents, my sisters, and my grandfather, watching and smiling. I wave to them, to let them know that I appreciate their pride and adoration that I am now participating in a meaningful, albeit pretty much decided, contest.

So engrossed am I, basking in the glow of my status as an official on-the-field-during-an-actual-game player, that my mind somehow fails to register the sound of a piece of wood connecting with a baseball. No, I am still watching the crowd, and I see them rise almost as one, and they are looking in my direction! AT ME! Billy Rutherford -Left Fielder! I see all of this but, about a second later, out of the corner of my eye, I also see a white blur streaking overhead to my left. The crowd is now not only on their feet, but they are all screaming! My coach and the other players are pointing at me and yelling "THE BALL! THE BALL!"

It now dawns on me that the sound I heard, and the resulting white blur, was actually the baseball being hit over my head, dropping behind me, and rolling almost to the back fence. Jack Long is almost apoplectic as he screams for me to "GET THE BALL!!!!" I turn, race toward the back fence and, reaching the ball, I throw it as hard as I possibly can in the general direction of the infield. Remember at the beginning of this chapter when I said I lacked the ability to hit or catch the ball? I probably should have included that throwing the ball was not my strong suit either. The ball was airborne for approximately half the distance from me to second base when, fortunately, Tom Finnegan races out and scoops it up, turns and throws it to home plate, but not in time to stop the second run from scoring.

I thought the rest of the team, and everyone in the stands were going to storm the field and do me great bodily harm, but for some reason, they held back- apparently being much more law-abiding fans in the 50's than what exists today.

Somehow everyone settles down, and the inning continues. I am trying my best to avoid making eye contact with anyone- family, coaches, team members- literally anyone. Thankfully the next batter grounds out and the top of the inning is over. The score is now tied at 4-4. I am not sure if I should return to the bench, or beat a hasty retreat into the pine forest at the back of the field. I know that everyone is watching me, as I slowly make my way to the sidelines. Jack Long is still too upset to speak to me; my teammates are all casting murderous glances in my direction, and basically treating me like the leper in the group. As I take my usual and now probably permanent spot at the end of the bench, the player next to me, my cousin Pat, slides as far away from me as possible, apparently not wanting to be anywhere close to the "KID WHO BLEW THE BIG GAME!". I did not dare turn and look at my family, since I figured that they were already making plans to either send me to an orphanage, or take me out and abandon me in the woods outside of town to be devoured by the bears and wolves.

Fortunately, Bob Hill comes to the rescue, and blasts a lead-off home run over the center field fence at the bottom of the inning to give us a 5-4 lead and end the game. I am sure that his heroic hit not only saved Jack Long's coaching gig, but my life as well.

It took some time, but eventually people seemed to forgive and forget my baseball crime that almost robbed the town of its dignity, and I was once again able to walk the streets, and attend church and school without fearing for my life. My parents still allowed me to live in the same house with them, and my grandfather even let me continue to visit him. I should note that, even though I was on the team for a few more years, I never got in a game again, even if we were ahead by ten runs.

That team was not the first manifestation of baseball in town. There is mention of it in the very beginnings of the town back in the early 1900's. So, let's go back there now, and see how the town was born, grew, and almost died...

"*Timber-r-r-r-r-r-r!*"

"My name is Bill. I've never failed, and I never will."
-William S. "Big Bill" Winegar

While Winegar in the 1950's was a very small, quiet village, it wasn't always that way. Formed early in the 20th century, it once boasted a population of nearly 2000 residents, and had one of the largest logging operations in the northern part of the state.

The following account of the early history of Winegar is an excerpt taken, with permission, from the book "*Crab Lake Memories*" by Liza Tuttle:

When J.J. Foster first surveyed the area, his ambition was to establish a thriving business. Foster came to the Northwoods from Greenville, Michigan, in 1905, a time when the prospects for the lumber industry in the region seemed quite good. The virgin timber in the area included several desirable species of hardwoods, such as maple, ash, and white birch. But the most prized trees were huge, virgin white pines. Foster, as president of the Vilas County Lumber Company, hoped to make his fortune logging the timber and preparing it in his mill for the urban markets of cities such as Milwaukee, Chicago, and Minneapolis.

The successful exploitation of the forests in northern Wisconsin depended entirely on the railroad system that opened up the region in the late 1880s. Both the Chicago & North Western Railroad and the Chicago-Milwaukee-St. Paul Railroad had routes extending to small northern towns- Manitowish, and Mercer respectfully. The Chicago & North Western eventually built a spur line which ended in the turnabout at Fosterville. The railroad into town was primarily for transporting supplies and lumber company officials, but passengers were sometimes allowed.

A scene from the Fosterville Lumber Mill. Photo courtesy of Mr. Jack Winegar

As a starting point, the Vilas County history, written in 1924, gives a good overview of the area's general history. Foster built his sawmill and began logging in 1905, but was unable to manage the venture successfully and gave up in 1910. The company found another man, William S. Winegar, of Grand Rapids, Michigan, to superintend the business.

Winegar was described in the Vilas County history as a man of "abundant energy" who turned around the fortunes of the Fosterville mill. The history reads: "the result of his labors may be seen in the present plant and village, presenting one of the most active industrial scenes in Vilas County." Winegar renamed the village after himself, claiming due credit for his successful efforts. In 1955, well after the mill was gone, the town was renamed Presque Isle.

The early settlers of Winegar experienced the unusual circumstances of a company-controlled town. Perhaps the influence of the company on the lives of the residents helped them to feel unified and protected. The company employed most of the men in town. It owned the houses that the families lived in, and even chose the color that the dwellings would be painted. It regulated the use of electricity, shutting it off completely for eight hours each day. The company printed its own currency with which it paid its employees, money that could only be spent in the company store, the company recreation hall, and other establishments within the town limits.

Clarence Childers, who lived in Winegar for most of his life, details for us what life was like in the mill, and the town, during its heyday:

"When I worked at the sawmill, I worked on the grounds outside. I didn't want to work inside. You were pushed by steam, and you had to go, go, go. It was pretty dangerous in there, especially early on. Eventually, after more and more people got hurt, they had to put in some safety devices. The logs came one right after another, and you just didn't get behind. If you got real behind, the guys up front would take five. But you really tried hard to keep up.

"Winegar, the man, didn't stay around much. You know them guys with money, they don't have to stand there, they got men to do that. He'd go to Florida or somewhere. There was a foreman for the lumberyard, and one for the mill. Then there was a superintendent of the woods; he kept charge over all the camps. There were at least six camps. The railroad spur trains were the link between them. The cars would go off empty in the morning, each to a different camp, and they'd come back with a full load later. They had three engines, geared down so they were built for power, not speed.

"Your lumberjacks, they weren't in town much, maybe on weekends only. But in the spring of the year, when the horses couldn't get out in the woods because it was too wet, they'd shut down the woods for about a month. All those guys would come to town, and the money they'd saved up all winter long, they'd blow it all in two weeks. They'd just drink it up. They'd get drunk and spill it all over- tens, twenties. As long as they had something to eat and something to wear, they didn't care about money. I remember when they would come into the pool hall. There were a lot of husky guys, of all different nationalities- Poles, Russians, Swedes. Cora Spencer used to make moonshine, you know, and they'd go buy themselves a jug, and go down and drink. She'd make up a stew for them, they'd eat it and go back to drinking, until all their money was used up. Then back to the woods, working and slaving. That was hard work in those days.

"There was an awful lot of moonshining in the Prohibition days. Finally, all the big guys in town decided they was going to clean up the town, get rid of all those goldarn Kentucks; raise heck with them. The superintendent of the mill, a big fat man, and a small, cocky town constable both got a month off with full pay to track down the moonshiners and arrest them.

"They'd have to take the moonshiners in to Eagle River because it was a federal offense. One time Cora got arrested, but she made such good moonshine that they got drunk on the way to Eagle River. They drank up all the evidence and got a good buzz on. After that, they didn't want to bust up her still.

"These railroad cars that came in from the woods, they'd come in a string of 25-30 cars, and the men would unload 'em. When they had more than the mill could handle, they'd deck 'em- pile them up on the side of the pond. The "hot pond" we called it. It got full quick. When there wasn't much coming in, they'd use up the logs in the pile. On the other side of the mill was the wood yard, where all the finishing work was done.

"The mill had a huge electric generator that furnished electricity for the whole town. At night, they'd flash the lights, and you had 15 minutes to get ready for bed, or else you'd be doing everything in the dark. The lights would go back on again between 5am and 6am, so for seven to eight hours, you didn't have any lights.

The train depot at Fosterville- Photo courtesy of Mr. Jack Winegar

"We had dances above the pool hall almost every other Saturday night. People would come from nearby towns, and they'd have orchestras come in from Chicago or Milwaukee. People would donate money, and the guys would play as long as they wanted to play, and they'd pass a hat around if people wanted them to keep playing. We had movies up there too, silent ones, once a week, and it was a big deal. The place would be packed.

"And if the lumberjacks were in town there'd be a real scene. They had to have someone in there to keep order over the kids, and the lumberjacks got a big kick out of the kids. They'd get a bunch of change- $20-$25 worth- and when they had to change the reels, they'd take a handful and throw it up against the stage, and the kids would scramble for the money. The lumberjacks got a big bang out of that; they'd just laugh and laugh. They'd do it every time they changed reels. Then they'd have a heck of a time getting them kids settled down again.

"Sometimes the lumberjacks would get into fights among themselves. They'd just get in an argument over something and there'd be bloody battles. I used to have to clean the floor in front of the bar. The pool hall was the only tavern in town, with three full-sized pool tables. On weekends and on paydays those tables would be going, game after game. There were also five or six slot machines, and a player piano. I used to clean up the place, and packed ice around the coils to keep the beer cold, and keep the icebox full of ice. I sold newspapers, and also shined shoes in front of the barber shop that was in the back of the pool hall. I picked up quite a few bucks, about $25 a week doing that. That was a lot of money back then. Heck, a movie only cost us 20 cents. On a dance night, the guys would be lined up for a shoe shine. They'd want to look nice. Guys from the boarding house, lots of single guys from Ironwood and all over, that were working at the sawmill. They had a ball team too, and they'd give the good players from other towns a cushy job at the mill, so they could keep them to play ball on Sundays, every Sunday at the diamond.

"When World War I broke out William Winegar had just bought the mill, and for a long time the guys worked but they got no pay. So Winegar called a big meeting, and told everyone not to worry about their money, they'd get that, but he needed cash to pay for the mill. He kept right on running when all the mills in the area were shutting down. He was one of the main suppliers of lumber, and he paid his men off when he hit the jackpot. He was the only one in the area that had any dry lumber. They'd run all day long, up until 9 o'clock at night. Of course, lots of men in town went to war, too.

During Prohibition, moonshining in the town was an occupation respected by most residents. Court dockets contain numerous cases of residents who "did unlawfully have in their possession for the purpose of sale, and did then and there unlawfully sell, vend, deal, and traffic in, and for the purpose of evading the law, did then and there unlawfully give away certain intoxicating liquors, the same, then and there being known as 'moonshine' and then and there being unlawfully privately manufactured distilled intoxicating liquors, contrary to the statues and laws of the state of Wisconsin"

Some of the moonshiners came to the area from Kentucky, and the Kentuckian faction knew the moonshining trade very well. Their families built stills in the forest behind the town and the tried and true recipes they used produced plenty of liquor to keep everyone happy. Residents of the town later stated that, at one time in Winegar, you could knock on almost any door in town and make a deal for some moonshine. That is, until the mill managers took it upon themselves to crack down on the trade.

The company paid a few supervisors to enforce Prohibition in Winegar, and "to get rid of them goldarn Kentucks" who made moonshine so well. Some might call the company actions intrusions into employee privacy. And yet, when Winegar asked his laborers to continue working without pay until the end of World War I, they did. The company took care of things, and the townspeople seemed very loyal in return. However, as you will see next, this crackdown on the moonshiners led to a violent confrontation that no one expected....

Winegar Massacre

"The mill company did not take kindly to moonshining. For some reason, neither did the local chapter of the Ku Klux Klan, which had sprung up around Winegar and was surprisingly powerful."

The following article was originally published in the *Lakeland Times* newspaper on August 12th, 1976. It marked the 50th anniversary of one of the bloodiest events in the town's history. One of the men murdered that day was my great-uncle, George Rutherford. Here is how it happened:

"Winegar Massacre Took Place 50 Years Ago Today"

Fifty years ago today, on August 12th, 1926, the area around Presque Isle, or Winegar as it was then called, rang with the gunshots of two separate, but related clashes, that left a total of five men dead or wounded.

Though the John Dillinger shootout that would occur eight years later was destined to become much more celebrated in

Northwoods legend, the little known events of August 12th, 1926, probably made that day the bloodiest, most violent day in the history of the Lakeland area, even a Lakeland area that was used to spurts of vigilante or frontier justice in the 1920's, when hastily deputized lawmen or hastily authorized posses' had little awareness of "due process", and shot first and asked questions later.

Winegar in prohibition era 1926 was a busy sawmill town, employing many men in town and even more in the logging camps outside. The hilly countryside, somewhat akin to their native Kentucky, had attracted a number of Kentuckians- "Kentucks" they were locally called- and a few of the Kentucks had found the privacy of these hills an ideal place to practice an art that had brought them from their Appalachian hill-home: Moonshining.

The mill company did not take kindly to this moonshining. For some reason, neither did the local chapter of the Ku Klux Klan, which had sprung up around Winegar and was surprisingly powerful.

That fateful Thursday afternoon, George Rutherford, a lumber company locomotive engineer, part time Methodist preacher, Ku Klux Klan leader, and for five months now, the local constable, hiked out toward one of the stills on the southwest corner of Mermaid Lake. He had his wife with him.

Reports still vary today about the reason for his errand; whether he was going out to serve an arrest warrant on murder fugitive William Stanley, whom he expected to find and reportedly may have arrested before, only to have him escape, or whether he had been promised a week's vacation by the mill superintendent if he closed down the Mermaid Lake still, and was on his way to do that.

Seeing smoke and hearing the sounds from afar of wood-chopping and closer of a fire crackling, Rutherford loaded his rifle, told his wife to wait, and stole the 85 feet to the still, which was situated in a little 16 by 20 foot clearing. He eluded the sentry or two that apparently had been stationed at the clearing, one Jerry Brandenburg, and perhaps William Stanley.

Just pulling the fire from the still, or getting ready to make the moonshine, was Charles Boring. Seeing Rutherford, he grabbed for the gun he kept handy. Spotting Boring's quick move, the constable ordered "Give me your gun!" and repeated "Give me that gun!"

As he repeated himself, in probably what was the last sentence he was ever to speak, he shot Boring in the hand as Boring made for his gun.

Boring shot back twice, one bullet blasting out much of Rutherford's brain after boring in just three-quarters of an inch above the left eye. "I seen him," Mrs. Rutherford swore at Boring's trial, recounting Boring shooting her husband. Then the new widow ran for help, first to a nearby cottage, and then on to town, a mile and a half away.

At that cottage, on her return with the doctor, she encountered Boring. Now joined by Brandenburg, Boring had begun fleeing west, but had doubled back to the cabin, perhaps because of the serious hand wound he had incurred. In court, Mrs. Rutherford described the hand as having "quite a big hole and swelled up." She asked him if he shot George. He said "No".

The doctor meanwhile proceeded to the clearing to find the body and pronounce Rutherford dead. Then he treated Boring's hand, and Boring was taken to town.

A couple of hours passed before a small posse of sorts was commissioned and got underway, to search for the watchers who had got away from the scene at the still. The two amateur lawmen comprising the posse, (Elmer Monk and "Big Alix" Garas) lay in wait down in a ditch near Jerry Brandenburg's farmhouse. When they heard familiar voices up on the road, posse-man Monk flashed his flashlight on their owners in the fog and semi-darkness and ordered them to halt.

Brandenburg, according to testimony at his trial, fired five shots at Monk, the wielder of the flashlight, before Monk managed to give Brandenburg a face full of buckshot at point-blank range. Both men fell, Brandenburg to lie there until someone came to find him in the morning, in the ditch, almost as an afterthought. Still alive, he was taken into custody.

With Brandenburg, and now so desperate to get out of the county that he had shortly before threatened to kill him if Brandenburg didn't get him out, was William Stanley, the fugitive wanted back in Kentucky on a charge of murdering a 25 year old deputy constable in Barrett, Kentucky, some months earlier.

"Big Alix" Garas' deposition in the assault trial of Brandenburg for shooting the deputized Monk, tells what was happening between Garas and Stanley as Monk and Brandenburg were tangling: "I shot Stanley and he fell ("resisting arrest", according to his death certificate) just as he had his gun up to shoot at Elmer. Stanley fell without shooting at all. As he went down, Stanley said "I am killed," and he never moved anymore."

Its climax had passed but the day's drama was not quite played out. "Big Alix" went to a house on a nearby farm for help for his injured partner. The court record gives the name as Passicks' house on Dr. Pinch's farm.

In a display of merciless pettiness that has rarely been surpassed in the normally big-hearted Lakeland area, Passick refused to aid the stoic Monk, whose only recorded complaint about his wounds was, "Don't touch my arm. I guess I lost my eye too" Not only that, but the farmhouse tenant refused to even let Garas leave the critically ill Monk there while he went elsewhere for help. "No," he said, according to the testimony on record. "You can't leave him in my yard. Take him out in the road." He surled. Then he shut the gate and went in the house, Garas's deposition concluded.

In Winegar, the electric mood did not subside quickly. A makeshift hospital room was fitted to house Monk, while another room across the hall served as a morgue for autopsies on Rutherford and Stanley the next day.

It was, by now, Friday the thirteenth, and outside, angry townspeople milled about, seething for revenge, according to papers as far away as Milwaukee, which went on to say that the crowds still thirsted to lynch the man who had shot George Rutherford.

On the highest knob of Winegar's brand-new cemetery, the martyred Rutherford's new grave initiated the new burial ground, and his friends buried him facing southward, so he could face the spot where he had died.

Miraculously, due process appeared out of the shambles, and dusted itself off. Two trials were held in Eagle River (the county seat) 60 days later. Boring, claiming that the Klan had sent the constable after him, that the Klan was bent on seeing him convicted and, that he could not get a fair trial in Vilas County because of the Klan's strength there, asked for a change of venue.

It was denied, but under that pressure, every single prospective juror was so carefully questioned about possible familiarity with, or ties to, the Klan, that the record of the examination of prospective jurors is one of the most massive sections of the trial record!

Charles Boring received life in prison for the murder of George Rutherford from a court that felt there was no validity to his claim of self-defense, since he had a right to expect a surprise arrest at any time he was moonshining. Jerry Brandenburg received a shorter term for getting the deputy in the eye; a charge in connection with harboring the fugitive/felon Stanley was dropped or plea bargained, along with a charge stemming from the afternoon shooting at the still.

Even a long a time after the shootings, the Klan still struck fear into some of the parties. Fears of reprisal by the Klan heightened the tension, along with fears that revenge seekers, especially kin or associates of Stanley's, might journey up from Kentucky to get even with his slayers.

"Big Alix" reportedly lived for years in fear for his life, and ironically he did die by gunshot in an argument with the fellow he lived with, 32 years after the shootouts of 1926. In the book, "Crab Lake Memories", Clarence Childers describes what became of "Big Alix":

"The cop who killed Stanley, his name was Alix, and he died the same way Stanley did. He got shot in an incident years later. He was living out in the woods with an old guy named Matt Anderson, and they were on a big drunk, you see.

They probably got into an argument and ol' Matt, he shot Alix. "Matt finally sobered up and came into town a couple of days later. He went to Lucille Eschenbauch's place and said "Hey, I guess maybe you better send someone out there. Me and Alix got in a fight, and I shot him. He's just layin' there and I'm getting' tired of walkin' over him. I guess he must be dead." Matt never even got sent to prison for that. He was drunk; maybe it was self-defense; who knows?"

As we referenced in the beginning of this chapter, eight years after this shoot-out, a much more famous confrontation took place just ten miles away, at Little Bohemia Lodge, in Manitowish Waters, WI...

Bullets and Bloodshed
at Little Bohemia

"From September 1933 until July 1934, John Dillinger, and his violent gang, terrorized the Midwest, killing 10 men, wounding 7 others, robbing banks and police arsenals, and staging 3 jail breaks—killing a sheriff during one and wounding 2 guards in another."
-Federal Bureau of Investigation

From the Federal Bureau of Investigation's *"Famous Cases and Criminals"* webpage, we get the following information about the shoot-out at Little Bohemia Lodge, in Manitowish Waters:

During the 1930s Depression, many Americans, nearly helpless against forces they didn't understand, made heroes of outlaws who took what they wanted at gunpoint. Of all the lurid desperadoes, one man, John Herbert Dillinger, came to evoke this Gangster Era and stirred mass emotion to a degree rarely seen in this country.

Dillinger, whose name once dominated the headlines, was a notorious and vicious thief. From September 1933 until July 1934, he and his violent gang terrorized the Midwest, killing 10 men, wounding 7 others, robbing banks and police arsenals, and staging 3 jail breaks—killing a sheriff during one and wounding 2 guards in another.

The FBI had received a tip that there had been a sudden influx of rather suspicious guests at the summer resort of Little Bohemia Lodge, about 50 miles north of Rhinelander, Wisconsin. One of them sounded like John Dillinger and another like Baby Face Nelson.

From Rhinelander, an FBI task force set out by car for Little Bohemia. Two of the rented cars broke down enroute and, in the uncommonly cold April weather, some of the agents had to make the trip standing on the running boards of the other cars. Two miles from the resort, the car lights were turned off and the posse proceeded through the darkness. When the cars reached the resort, dogs began barking. The agents spread out to surround the lodge and as they approached, machine gun fire rattled down on them from the roof. Swiftly, the agents took cover. One of them hurried to a telephone to give directions to additional agents who had arrived in Rhinelander to back up the operation.

While the agent was telephoning, the operator broke in to tell him there was trouble at another cottage about two miles away. Special Agent W. Carter Baum, another FBI man, and a constable went there and found a parked car which the constable recognized as belonging to a local resident. They pulled up and identified themselves.

Inside the other car, Baby Face Nelson was holding three local residents at gunpoint. He turned, leveled a revolver at the lawmen's car and ordered them to step out. But without waiting for them to comply, Nelson opened fire. Baum was killed, and the constable and the other agent were severely wounded. Nelson jumped into the Ford they had been using and fled.

When the firing had subsided at the Little Bohemia Lodge, Dillinger was gone. When the agents entered the lodge the next morning, they found only three frightened females. Dillinger and five others had fled through a back window before the agents surrounded the house.

In his book, "*Gangster Holiday's: The Lore and Legend of the Bad Guys*", published in 1989, author Tom Hollatz gives us a version of the story that doesn't cast the Feds in the same glowing light:

"Dillinger was making the Feds look like fools. Not only was he pulling off many jobs, but was escaping right from under the noses of everyone…time and time again. It had been expected that once the FBI got into the action, that Dillinger would have just about held up his hands and begged for mercy. That didn't exactly happen. Instead, Dillinger's crime spree seemed to be escalating.

"What happened one night at Little Bohemia Lodge in Manitowish Waters would become part of American lore, forever carving Dillinger's name in a gangster litany of sorts that belongs to the ages.

"The entire "get Dillinger" scenario began to take form on Sunday, April 22nd, 1934, when two planes from Chicago touched down at the Rhinelander airport. Aboard were Melvin Purvis and other FBI agents. The plane from the St. Paul bureau was already on the ground. It carried Assistant Director H. Hugh Clegg, who was now counting his troops, some 17 in all. Local wardens and constables would be added later when the Dillinger dragnet was triggered.

"Clegg was first in command, and Purvis second. One agent returned with Henry Voss to his resort, which would be used as the staging area for the attack. Later, the remaining agents followed in rented cars, turning north at Woodruff on Highway 51.

"The plan was for Emil Wanatka Sr., the owner of Little Bohemia Resort, to herd whoever was inside the building into the basement at about 4:00 am. It was hoped other Feds would have had time to drive from St. Paul to block roads before the assault. But word had gotten out that Dillinger planned to leave after dinner on Sunday night and not on the 23rd as the Feds hoped. They rushed to adjust their plans.

"It was a cold trip out of Rhinelander in the five cars. When two of the clunkers broke down, several agents climbed on running boards. Armed with an assortment of weapons, it was no easy task, especially on that frigid night. The road was muddy; deep holes made it a difficult trip.

"At Birchwood Lodge, Voss's resort on Highway 51 near Little Bohemia, Clegg organized his men for a quick assault, fearing Dillinger was going to flee, and soon.

"The agents set out in three cars with all lights out- and all cigarettes were doused. They headed northwest on Highway 51.

"At the entrance to Little Bohemia, a good distance from the main lodge on Little Star Lake, Clegg ordered two of the cars to block the entrance in a V formation.

Ít should be pointed out that the Feds were totally unfamiliar with Little Bohemia. Voss scribbled a map that left out three main factors:

1. There was a ditch to the left of the lodge.
2. There was a fence to the right.
3. There was a steep bank near the lake. Because of the steepness it provided a perfect shield and cover for anyone who walked- or ran- along the shoreline.

"Inside, Dillinger was playing cards with his men in the bar. Outside, the Wanatkas' two collies started barking. Something in the darkness sparked their yelping. Dillinger didn't even look up.

"Three local diners, a gas station attendant from Mercer and two men from the CCC camp, decided to leave. Inside the noisy car, augmented by a crackling loud radio, the three men felt good after the $1.00 Sunday night chicken dinner, a favorite offering of the Wanatkas.

"The dogs continued barking. Bartenders Frank Traube and George Bazso stepped outside to see what, if anything, was causing the dogs to bark.

"The agents watched as the three men entered the car and Traube and Bazso stood at one side. Seeing five men emerge, the agents thought it was an alerted Dillinger and his gang, ready to flee. They got ready.

"The car carrying John Hoffman, the gas station attendant, John Morris, a CCC cook, and Eugene Boiseneau, a CCC specialist, drove slowly along the long pine tree-lined entrance to Highway 51. The car's lights bounced through the blackness as the wheels found the frequent potholes.

"Fearing the gang was trying to escape, Clegg and Purvis ordered their men to open fire- first at the tires. The three occupants of the car did not hear the command to "halt," and the car continued to move.

"It was then that all hell broke loose as the agents, using .38's and Thompson submachine guns, fired at will.

"John Morris, hit four times by FBI bullets, spilled from the passenger side of the car. Shaking in terror, he fled back to the lodge. Morris grabbed the bar phone and called Alvin Koerner. "Alvin, I'm at Emil's. Everybody here has been knocked out." With that Morris collapsed.

"Hoffman, also wounded, stumbled from the driver's side and crawled to the safety of the nearby woods. Slumped in the middle seat was Gene Boiseneau, age 35. He was staring straight ahead at the blood-drenched dashboard, killed instantly in the first volley.

"Inside, Dillinger and his men scrambled away with precision.

"Lester M. Gillis, aka Baby Face Nelson, in a nearby cabin with his wife, stayed a few moments, reportedly firing two pistols at a figure with a submachine gun, believed to be Purvis. He missed. Purvis' weapon jammed. Nelson ran for the lake, exchanging fire with Purvis, now using a .38. Nelson escaped down the steep hill and along the shoreline.

"Wanatka, and the three gangster molls left behind, scrambled for the basement. The girls would remain there until the following morning, Clegg ordered a ceasefire. In the madness of the assault some agents, who were flanking Little Bohemia, fell into the ditch on the left. Those on the right ran into the barbed wire fence. It was chaos.

"It would be several hours before the Feds would teargas the lodge and then break in. A somewhat befuddled Purvis, who would later commit suicide, for some reason would not believe Emil

Wanatka Sr., who had been at Alvin Koerner's when Nelson unleashed his terror on agents W. Carter Baum and Jay Newman. Constable Carl Christensen was also struck in that momentary fury.

"It was over.

"Dillinger and his men were gone.

"The public outcry was just beginning. What would follow would be the most intense manhunt by the Feds in United States history.

"The reign of terror across the nation that Dillinger waged was ended on July 22, 1934. At 10:30 pm that night, John Dillinger was shot and killed by federal agents as he left the Biograph Theater in Chicago, accompanied by the famous "Lady in Red", Anna Sage, who had tipped off the FBI to the location of Public Enemy No. 1. Her reward for helping the Feds- she was deported to her native Romania, where she died in 1947. FBI agent, Melvin Purvis, was so tormented by J. Edgar Hoover's treatment of Ms. Sage that he took his own life in 1960.

"Baby Face Nelson was killed in a savage gun duel on Northwest Highway in Barrington, IL, on November 27th of that year. It was said to be one of the fiercest gun battles ever waged between lawmen and gangsters.

Wow! That was a lot of bullets and bloodshed! While we wait for the gun smoke to clear and for them to remove the bodies and patch up the bullet holes at Little Bohemia, let's head back over to Winegar where, unfortunately, the town itself seemed to be dying....

Death Knell for a Small Town

"We hope that someday Winegar may be as it formerly was but, of course, there is no need to look forward to this, for it is too far gone."

-Velma Kunschke

All the towns within the county, owing their origin to the lumber industry, were themselves subject to its transient nature, flourishing while lumber and manpower were abundant, then coming to a standstill once all the timber in the area was cut. Mills were eventually shut down and most of the population moved elsewhere.

This excerpt from the county history predicted almost exactly the fate of Winegar:

"Phelps and Winegar, both present time good-size and flourishing villages, are also lumber mill towns and the respective headquarters of logging operations. To eliminate the lumber industry from either would mean it's immediate reduction to a very small hamlet, or possibly it's total extinction."

The following interviews, from *"Crab Lake Memories"*, with Clarence Childers, Lucille Eschenbauch, and Velma Kunschke, tell the story of the end of the logging business.

Clarence- "The mill's all gone now. After they got the whole area all logged out, they had no choice. They cleared everything except the little trees. There was no such thing as selective logging. They didn't even bother to clean up all the branches and everything. Then someone would come in and set it all on fire. I remember in the late 30's a fire got out of control and the town was surrounded by flames. We were all set to evacuate, but we never had to."

"They took down the pool hall eventually. The building got old, and it was condemned. When the mill went out, you didn't have any lumberjacks, and there just wasn't any money. Then it was torn down, and the lumber was used for a tavern that went up across the street. That was Gunnar Larson's. He used to be busier than the dickens. Then all kinds of them started up. A bar always gets business up here."

Lucille-"I don't think people in town thought the lumber in the area would ever be depleted. They thought it would last forever and ever. When you are working for your room and board, you don't think of that. You just keep going. I think it was the company's fault. They should have done like Weyerhauser out in Washington, and replanted a tree every time they cut one. Instead, they clear cut the entire area.

In her memoir, apparently told in the 1930's, Velma describes how the town suffered when the logging ran out:

"Mr. Bonifas, and Joe Gorman bought the company in 1926. Because the wages were so little, Winegar has been decreasing rapidly.

Last year and this year people have moved until the population has decreased to one-half the amount it formerly was. Practically the whole town is receiving relief (welfare) because there is no work whatever for them.

"Last spring most of the mill machinery and lumber was moved to Lake Linden (north of Houghton, MI), by trucks.

"No families from other cities would want to move here, because the streets and yards are so untidy, and the houses are practically ruined. All interest seems to have been lost in the upkeep of Winegar, which has a great deal to do with the downfall. Tourists no longer desire to come here because of these reasons.

"We hope that someday Winegar may be as it formerly was but, of course, there is no need to look forward to this, for it is too far gone."

But the town didn't die, as other logging communities did, when the timber ran out and the mills closed. Even though they struggled mightily to eke out a living, the people did not give up. The town now focused on the one thing that could possibly sustain it- tourism.

In the 1920's and 1930's residents had already begun to develop a summer resort business, in an effort to establish a new and hopefully permanent prosperity. At the time County Road W was the only route into town, and County Road B was just a fire lane. Tourists would have to leave their cars in town, be met by a guide, and be transported by canoe, boat, or horse-drawn wagon to local resorts and summer homes. As both the roads and the town services improved, the vacation industry increased, so that by the late 1950's there were well over twenty resorts in operation, all vying for their share of the tourism dollars.

Commercial development in the 1950's was great enough that the first Chamber of Commerce was formed. The township now boasted three grocery stores, two gas stations, a combination restaurant and souvenir shop, two hardware stores, two churches, a summer bakery, and approximately ten taverns.

A new school had been built at the top of the hill on the north end of Main Street. Its impact on the town was immediate and long lasting, as you will see....

Readin', Writin', and 'Rithmetic...

"The school had just been built and it was the pride of the community"

-Janis Felts

Built in 1939, the town school was originally called the Winegar State Graded School, but was more commonly known, in later years anyway, as the Presque Isle Grade School. It was a somewhat massive building for such a small town, and it was certainly built to last.

The new Presque Isle Grade School, located just across from the Red and White Store. This picture was taken just after the school opened in 1939-40. Photo courtesy of Ms. Janis Felts.

The school had two classrooms, both on the upper floor; the lower grades, one through four were in what was known as the "Little Room" and the upper grades, fifth through eighth, were in the "Big Room".

Also on that floor was the office/library, and a hallway that led to the north entrance of the building. Downstairs was the gym, the kitchen and lunchroom, bathrooms and showers, and the furnace room. (the furnace room was also the unofficial smoking room for students, and even one or two teachers)

Some may say that this classroom set-up wasn't very good, since the teacher had to teach different subjects at different grade levels throughout the day. With 15-20 students in each room, there were probably 3-6 children in each grade. So, if the teacher was teaching 5th grade math, for example, those 5th grade students would report to the front of the room and sit in a row of chairs placed there. The rest of the students would remain at their regular desks, until it was their grade's turn in front. When that subject was done the teacher would call up the next group for whatever subject they were to be taught.

While the individual students didn't get nearly as much face time with the teacher as students in today's school, they actually were much better taught. You see, while they were at their desks doing their school work, they all had the opportunity to see and hear what was being taught in the front of the room. So fifth graders, during the course of the day, would not only go thru their lessons with the teacher, they would be exposed to what the 6th, 7th, and 8th graders were learning!

It worked the same way in the lower grades, in the Little Room. First graders were able to listen and absorb spelling, math, and reading skills that were being taught to the grades ahead of them. In my opinion, and in the opinion of many others who attended that school, this was a huge learning advantage. I can honestly say that I probably learned as much in my five years of attending that little grade school in that tiny town, as some high school students are learning today.

Another huge advantage to this type of schooling is that I don't ever remember having homework. We had plenty of time during the school day to complete the assignments given to us. When school was over, it was play time! Today, I see my grandkids lugging heavy backpacks filled with books, and having to spend two hours a night doing homework. This would be in addition to practices for soccer, volleyball, basketball, etc…. kids today don't have enough downtime.

Clara Perron echoes that sentiment:

"Having more than one grade in a room, I always learned what the grade ahead of me learned. It was so much easier, like taking a class for 2 years. "I started first grade there, and I believe my teacher was Helen Larson. She lived with Mrs. McKenzie (or Mrs Mac, as everyone called her. Helen Larson (we called her Miss Larson), was really a wonderful teacher. Her handwriting was perfect, as were her numbers."

Janis Felts remembers going to the brand new school;

"I started school at age six; there was no kindergarten at that time. In the first grade I had Miss Larson, a beloved teacher who taught the lower grades, for many years. I can remember that she always wore a dark dress and managed to have a hankie tucked in a pocket. She always wore earrings. Miss Larson used to go outside with us and, in the spring, jumping rope was a must! We would coax her and she was a good sport and jumped rope with us.

"Some of the other teachers I had were the Bernsteins, Joyce Bowers, who was from Marenisco, Mr. Piersall, and Veryl Wolhaupt. I don't remember if school lunch was served when the school first started, but we did have hot lunches eventually. Mr. DePressles was our first cook, and I believe Verna Spencer did the cooking at one time also. I certainly remember when our dear family friend, Margaret Tice, was the cook. We usually had one hot dish or soup, and a peanut butter and jelly sandwich with milk and cookies. One of my favorites, and I still make it occasionally, was creamed peas with chopped hard boiled eggs over mashed potatoes.

"One time we had navy bean soup, and there were little white things that were floating around in the bowl too. We all thought they were worms! Our teacher told us that those were common when cooking dried beans and they were not worms. However, we made such a fuss over it that poor Margaret started crying, and we all had to apologize to her!

"The gymnasium was used like a community room. There were basket socials, bingo games, card parties and the like. The town had a men's basketball team (one of the stars was Chet Dumask) that played teams from surrounding towns like Lac Du Flambeau, Marenisco, and Wakefield. At Christmastime, the school janitor and the townsfolk would put up a stage for the school Christmas program. Sometimes they would put on talent shows, and lots of town residents showed off their talents."

The school operated in this fashion at least up thru the 1960's to my knowledge. When I started there in 1956, I had Mrs. Marie Long as one of my teachers. Later on I had Mr. Piersall for one year, and in the fifth grade (my last year there), the teacher was Mr. Soami.

One year (I believe I was in second or third grade) the school only had one teacher, Mr. Piersall. That was the year we combined the classes and had all eight grades in one room. I remember my sister Cindy coming home and telling my mother "Mom! The teacher said I was the smartest girl in the fifth grade!" To which my mom jokingly replied "Don't let it go to your head. There's only you and Johnny Eschenbauch in the fifth grade.!" The next year we went back to having two classrooms.

As I recall, Mr. Piersall was fairly strict, and not a lot of the kids liked him, especially the older boys. Since there was no housing available for him, he actually lived at the school, which was alright, since it did have everything he needed (kitchen, bathroom, a room to sleep in), and it was free. I mentioned that some of the older boys didn't like Mr. Piersall, and they decided to get even with him for being so strict with them.

Mr. Piersall owned a gray Plymouth that he parked out behind the school. One morning he came out and found that all four tires had been removed and his car now rested on cement blocks. The tires were nowhere to be found, although they did turn up later, hidden in the pine trees that bordered the school lot. I don't know who came up with the plan, and no one would ever admit to being involved in the plot but, I personally know one of the culprits, even though, to this day, he maintains his innocence, albeit with a knowing smirk.

We had a boys' basketball team, and we played against Boulder Junction, Woodruff, and Marenisco. I wasn't on the team (my athletic abilities in basketball were even worse than my baseball skills, as described in a previous chapter) but I enjoyed going to the games, and getting that bag of fresh popcorn and a bottle of cherry pop.

Carl Wolter said that the grade school had a baseball team when he was there, but it was mostly girls. When asked if he played on the team, he said "No, because my class was me and about eight girls. So I learned how to play Hopscotch, Jacks… I could play a mean game of Jacks…"

Unlike today, the school year never started until the day after Labor Day. We didn't shut down for two days of parent/teacher conference, but during the week of Thanksgiving there was a lot of boys absent. That was the week of the gun deer hunting season, and most of the boys were all out driving deer for their dads, uncles, and grandfathers. We got a two week Christmas vacation, and a week off for Easter, along with Good Friday as well. The school year always ended just before Memorial Day.

One thing we never had was "snow days". Today, if the mostly inaccurate weatherman – oh, excuse me- meteorologist, says there is going to be temperatures below zero, or more than 4 inches of snow in say, Milwaukee, all the schools close, all after school activities are cancelled and people are advised to "STAY IN YOUR HOMES! DO NOT GO OUT EXCEPT IN CASES OF EXTREME EMERGENCIES!"

In Presque Isle, it was possible to get a few inches of snow in MAY! And as for temperatures, well, minus 25 degrees only meant that you just bundled up a bit more, and walked to school like any other day. Of course, that was before the meteorologists invented "wind chill" Apparently, back then we didn't know how cold we actually were but, to our credit, we didn't care.

In the five years that I attended the school, there were many memorable instances, but here are a few that have stood out in my mind;

One day, for some unknown reason, Pat Finnegan brought a can of sauerkraut into the classroom. We were in the Big Room and had Mr. Soami as our teacher. While the details are somewhat fuzzy, I do remember that Pat got the can open, but then dropped it on the floor, sending a large puddle of smelly sauerkraut juice spreading down between two rows of desks. Oh man, how that reeked! Some of you may enjoy sauerkraut, and that's fine, but that amount of juice unleashed in a closed room, was just about unbearable. Most of us got an extra-long recess, as Mr. Soami, Pat, and a couple of eighth grade boys cleaned up the mess.

Another time, a man and his wife showed up to enroll two of their sons in the school. They had just moved to town, and brought their boys to class. One boy was in seventh grade, and the other was in eighth grade. I don't know where they went to school before that, but I can tell you that those two boys were not interested in attending the Presque Isle Grade School at all! Their parents had to literally wrestle both of them into the classroom, and finally were able to slam them into their seats, all while we watched. I can tell you that I have seen World Wresting Entertainment matches that were not as much fun as the five minutes of mayhem that unfolded that morning. Surprisingly, the boys settled down after that day and, as far as I knew, never caused any problems after that. (I am not using their names here since they are both still with us, and may be inclined to kick my ass for telling this story)

The most memorable event that took place during this time, happened in the winter of 1961. At that time, we probably only had about 25 or so students in the school. It was during recess that a group of the eighth graders made their way to a corner of the playground by themselves. Someone lit up a cigarette and they began passing it around. Suddenly, one of the kids spotted Mr. Soami making his way rapidly toward the group. The cigarette ended up being tossed down, where it landed in the middle of the smoking circle. When Mr. Soami demanded to know whose cigarette that was, everyone was suddenly struck with an amnesia epidemic, and no one could, or would, identify who belonged to the still smoldering butt. (It should be noted here that during a recent conversation I had with Bob Hill about this incident, he admitted being in the group, however swears he did not smoke and was unfairly considered one of the culprits)

Mr. Soami proceeded to march all eight of the kids into his office, and when none of them would tell him what he wanted to know, he ended up suspending every one of them! As far as I know, this large of a suspension had never happened before. My sister Cindy was one of those suspended. She went home and woke my dad, who had been working nights at the White Pine Copper Mine, in the U.P., and told him what happened. He said he would deal with it later, and went back to sleep.

While Mr. Soami was still in his office dealing with the students, Danny Peterson and I were busy entertaining the rest of the kids in the Big Room, by staging a pretend fight in the front of the classroom. Unfortunately for us, the hooting, hollering, and laughter of our fellow classmates, attracted the attention of Mr. Soami, who came to see what was going on. Needless to say, he was already in a foul mood from dealing with the smokers, and was not about to put up with any more nonsense. He simply pointed at Danny and I and said "Get out!" Tell your parents you are suspended!"

This was not good news for me, since I had never really been in any sort of trouble at school before. We tried apologizing to him, but Mr. Soami was adamant, and insisted we get out of his school right then. When I got home, Cindy was just sitting there looking miserable, and told me that Dad was still sleeping, and was not happy. But, I knew I had to tell him what had happened to me, so I went in and lightly shook his arm.

"WHAT?" he demanded as he rolled over and fixed me with a very, very angry look.

"Uh, Dad, I, uh, got sent home from school too..." I said quietly.

"What in the hell is going on at that damn school?" he asked, and since I was sure he wasn't really expecting me to answer, I didn't.

"Get out of here, and let me get some sleep!" he growled. "Your mom and I will take care of both of you after I get up!"

Cindy and I spent the rest of the afternoon being very quiet. Obviously both of us were plenty afraid of what our punishment was going to be, and we were dreading the moment when my mom came home, and we had to face the music.

Well, Mom came home, Dad woke up, we told them in detail what happened, and when they were done with us, sitting was more than a bit uncomfortable. Then, to make matters worse, we all had to go before a special session of the school board that night. Because so many kids (ten in all) had been suspended a meeting was called so the matter could be dealt with. I don't know what happened with the smokers, since we were each called in separately, but I know I was pretty embarrassed when it was my turn to stand before the adults. Mr. Soami explained why I was suspended, and then my mom spoke up and made me apologize to Mr. Soami, and tell the school board what my punishment had been. It was very humiliating to tell everyone about the spanking I had gotten just a few hours ago. I think I was wishing that the floor would open up and swallow me, but such a face-saving event was not in the cards. While I am sure that at least some of the other kids probably got spanked as well, I don't know they had to publicly admit it.

The evening finally ended with all of us being re-instated, and we returned to class the next morning. While I am sure that the smoking continued, no one was ever caught again, to my knowledge, and Danny and I never reenacted our fight again.

Joan McDonald tells us about the final chapter of the school:

"In the late 1960's, a decision was made to consolidate the grade schools from Presque Isle, Boulder Junction, Manitowish Waters, and Winchester. The new school was completed in 1970 and was located at the intersection of County Highways P and K. The site for the new school was chosen because that is the spot where the townships of Presque Isle, Boulder Junction, and Winchester all meet. The new school was called North Lakeland Elementary School.

"The new school is still being used today. It has been consolidated into a kindergarten through eighth grade. Elementary school consists of kindergarten through fourth grade and middle school is fifth grade thru eighth grade.

"After the school was moved to the new building, the old building became the town library. They also used the school for town meetings, 4H club, along with basket socials, and the town offices were also in that building. It remained that way until the building was torn down in 1994."

A final humorous note regarding the school's name- When the town changed its name from Winegar to Presque Isle in 1955, the school then became known as the "Presque Isle Grade School". A few years later, someone floated the idea that school rings should be made and given to the eighth graders at graduation. A great idea, but with one fatal flaw- the design. You see, most school rings don't have room on them for the entire school name, so initials are used. Since the town's school was named the "Presque Isle Grade School", the initials on the rings would have looked like this – "P.I.G.S". (not very flattering, to be sure!) Upon realizing this flaw, I believe the whole ring idea was scrapped, never to be brought up again.

Higher Learning

"The school bus, at times, would get stuck and the kids would have to get out and push."

Our school only went up to the eighth grade, after that the students were taken by bus over the state line to the high school in Marenisco, MI. Back in those days the road to Marenisco was, to say the least, as Janis Felts put it, "washboardy".

During the late 50's, Hwy M-64 was rebuilt, and that made the rides back and forth to school even more adventurous. The school bus at times would get stuck and the kids would have to get out and push. As Carl Wolter told me "If the bus got stuck in the morning and we had to push, we didn't put much effort into it because we weren't in any hurry to get to class. But if we got stuck on the way home, we all put our shoulders into it and got the bus unstuck as fast as possible…"

The bus rides also provided other opportunities for mischief, as Janis tells us;

"There was one morning when we got on the bus and a couple of boys pulled out a can of tobacco and three corn cob pipes! We were trying to keep it well hidden, and somehow they got the pipes filled and lit. We took turns puffing and some of the kids up front were laughing. Mr. McCloud was the driver at the time; a nice man. He kept looking in the rear view mirror and shaking his head. We didn't think he would report us and we were right. When we arrived at the school and got off the bus, he never said a word. But you know that there always had to be a "snitch" and, sure enough, not long after school started we were called up to the office and got a long chewing out. We still thought it was funny, but we never tried it again.

"There was also a budding romance during those bus rides. Caroline Hill and Frankie Jirikowic sat together every trip, back and forth. They got teased incessantly, but that relationship flourished and resulted in marriage and a beautiful family."

Janis graduated in 1952, and as she put it "Life's challenges were about to begin. Each of us took a different direction but, during that time, we experienced friendship, and comradery that enabled us to continue the road to adulthood."

My family moved away when I completed the fifth grade, so I didn't have the opportunity to attend high school in Marenisco. But back in Presque Isle, my education and learning experiences were not limited to just the nine months of the school year. During the course of one summer, I learned to speak in a different language- Latin!

Sunday Mass

Since we had not told anyone in town of my altar boy training, everyone who attended Mass that Sunday was taken by complete surprise as Fr. DeWitt followed me from the sacristy...

There are two churches in Presque Isle. At the end of Church Street, next to my grandfather's house, is the Bethel Lutheran Church. We lived in the house next to St. Rita's Catholic Church, on Lake Street, from 1955 until 1961. St. Rita's was a small, red brick building that was designed to hold approximately 100 worshippers (although the only time I can ever remember the church being filled to capacity was during funerals.) A large cross hung on the back wall above the altar, and a doorway on the right led to the sacristy. Statues of both the Virgin Mary and Joseph were on pedestals behind the Communion rail, which separated the Sanctuary from the two rows of pews. There were wooden kneelers in the pews but they lacked the padding that you find in churches today. During Sunday Mass, the women and children typically sat in the pews, while the men of the congregation stood in the back vestibule.

Masses were held on Sunday mornings at 9:00am, with the attending priest hearing confessions starting at 8 o'clock. One exception to this time was for funerals, which usually started with the viewing of the body in the vestibule at 9am and the Mass to follow at ten. (A quick note regarding funeral services- if you were Catholic your funeral was at St. Rita's, if you were Lutheran your funeral was held at Bethel, and if you were any other denomination, well then, your funeral service was held in the grade school gymnasium.) The only other exception for a change in the Mass schedule was for the two Sundays in November during deer hunting season. On those Sundays, Mass was celebrated at 5am so the men could attend services (in their hunting clothes) and still get out in the woods before dawn.

Since we were such a tiny community, we did not have a full-time priest assigned to our church. Therefore, the priest from either St. Anne's parish in Boulder Junction or St. Joseph's in Mercer came to our church to perform Mass.

On the other side of St. Rita's was a house that the church owned, and used as a rectory. It was common practice that priests from Wisconsin and Illinois could apply to use the rectory while on vacation. While there, they would be required to hear confessions, and perform the Sunday Mass; the rest of the time they were free to relax.

In 1958, a priest arrived in town to spend the summer. He was from Kankakee, Il, and his name was Fr. DeWitt. Now, one thing that Fr. DeWitt loved was mushrooms. He would spend hours in the woods around town picking mushrooms. As a matter of fact, in Kankakee, he was known as "The Mushroom Priest". He offered to split some of his bounty with my family but, since none of us shared his taste for fungi, we respectfully declined.

However, since we lived so close to each other, and I had nothing specific to do all summer, Fr. DeWitt and I became fast friends. I gladly accompanied him on his mushroom gathering trips, and when we came back, we usually stopped at the Lure for ice cream. He had been in town a few weeks when one day, while we were enjoying a root beer float, he asked me why there were no altar boys in town to help with Sunday Mass. I didn't know, and told him so. His response was,

"Well, why don't you be an altar boy?"

"I don't know how, Father."

"I'll teach you what to do, and what to say, and you can help me on Sundays. Ask your parents if they will allow it, and let me know. Otherwise, I will ask one of the other boys."

Thrilled at the idea of serving Mass, I ran home to tell my mom. She was more of a devout Catholic than my dad, and readily gave her permission. I ran to the rectory, and told Fr. DeWitt the good news.

"Great!" he exclaimed, "We will start your training in the morning!"

The next morning found me knocking on the rectory door bright and early. Fr. DeWitt let me in and, sitting at the kitchen table, he explained that the hardest part of being an altar boy was learning the prayers.

(At this point I should explain the difference between Catholic Masses in 1958, as opposed to the present day. The main difference was that, except for the Epistle, the Gospel, and the sermon, the entire Mass was in Latin. This meant that I had to learn all the prayers in Latin- which was not an easy task, I can assure you.)

Under Fr. DeWitt's patient instruction, it wasn't long before I was making significant progress. Some days we met in the rectory, other days we would practice while we were mushroom hunting; and then there were some nice days when we sat in the sun on the church steps and spent about an hour reciting the prayers, both his and mine, before we headed off to the woods to search for his beloved mushrooms. Once I had conquered the language of the Latin Mass, we would spend time in the church, going through the procedures and tasks that I would have to perform. It was important that I not only knew how to say the prayers correctly and loud enough, but also when to say them. In addition, I had to learn how and when to present the water and wine, when to ring the little bell that we used, and how to help with communion. (This was a lot for an eight-year old, but I was determined to learn all of it).

Nearly three weeks into my training, Fr. DeWitt declared that, in his opinion, I was ready to officially assume my duties as an altar boy. One Saturday morning, he called me over to the rectory and announced that I would be serving Mass the next day. I was both nervous and excited! I was even more surprised when Fr. DeWitt opened a package that he had at his side. Inside was a small black cassock, and a brilliant white surplice. I think my hands may have actually been shaking as I tried on those fine garments. He must have spoken with my mom and got my measurements, as the cassock was just the right length, and the surplice fit perfectly. I could hardly wait until Mass the next morning.

Since we had not told anyone in town of my altar boy training, everyone who attended Mass that Sunday was taken by complete surprise as Fr. DeWitt followed me from the sacristy. As we took our places in front of the altar, I could hear a few gasps, and lots of murmurs from the parishioners. At one point I was able to steal a glance at my family, sitting in the front pew, and saw that both my parents were wearing wide smiles. Later on, my sisters would tell me that mom had tears in her eyes, and dad looked proud as a peacock. As for me, my stomach was filled with butterflies but at the same time, I also felt an inner peace and confidence that I didn't know I possessed. I probably would have been much more nervous had we been facing the congregation, but the church had not yet made that change, so we faced the altar with our backs to the assembly.

The Mass begins, and I settled into my new role. We moved through the Anthem and onto the Confiteor:

"*Confíteor Deo omnipoténti, beátæ Maríæ semper Vírgini,......mea culpa, mea culpa, mea maxima culpa, etc....*

At that point I was very thankful for the hours of practice that Fr. DeWitt and I had put into my training. While the language was foreign to me, the words seemed to roll off my tongue effortlessly, and my confidence grew with each prayer.

After the *Kyrie* and the *Gloria*, I took my place, sitting on a chair by the left side of the sanctuary, while Fr. DeWitt read the *Epistle* and the *Gospel*. He then began his sermon by saying,

"As you can see, we have a new addition here at St. Rita's. Billy and I have been working very hard these last few weeks so he could become the very first altar boy in your church. I, along with his family, are very proud that he has accepted this honor to serve the Lord, and the parish of St. Rita's...."

The rest of the Mass went well, and I even avoided the common mistake that some altar boys make (sometimes intentionally) of banging the paten into the throats of those taking communion. Finally, the blessing is given and the Mass is over. Fr. DeWitt and I disappear into the sacristy, and he tells me that I did a terrific job. I thank him and, after carefully hanging my cassock and surplice in the small closet, I head out of church, where my family gathered around to give me hugs. It was a great moment!

There was a gentleman at the church, named Ray Sensenbrenner, who acted as caretaker and usher. Mr. Sensenbrenner came up to me after that first Mass, told me that he was so happy to see me up there serving Mass and, reaching in his pocket, pulled out two quarters and gave them to me. Now $.50, may not be anything today, but in 1958, to an eight-year old boy, that was a lot of money!! (Things got even better, as for the next several years, almost every time Mr. Sensenbrenner saw me, he gave me fifty cents. I am quite sure that if he were alive today, and saw me, he would smile, reach in his pocket, and give me four bits).

Two significant things happened after that initial Mass. The following Sunday I went to church; but instead of serving Mass, I sat in the pew with my family. When Fr. DeWitt got to the sermon he said, looking at me,

"I don't know what happened. Last week I had an altar boy, and this week I don't." He then proceeded to say the rest of the Mass by himself. When Mass was completed I made my way to the sacristy.

"Why didn't you serve Mass today?" Fr. DeWitt asked, not angry, but concerned.

"You never asked me too, Father." I responded.

He gave a chuckle and said "You are the only altar boy in this parish. It is now your responsibility to serve Mass every Sunday." I apologized for not being there and assured him that I would never miss another Mass. This proved to be incorrect, as I was about to have competition in the altar boy ranks....

Tom and Pat Finnegan, my two cousins, were also Catholic. Their mother, my Aunt Doris, was without a doubt the most religious woman in town, and was probably the only person in church that first Sunday who was not at all happy to see me up front with the priest during the service. The next day, she visited Fr. DeWitt at the rectory and convinced him that her two boys could easily learn the prayers and could also serve Mass. Fr. DeWitt, somewhat reluctantly, agreed to give them the same training he gave me, and it wasn't long before St. Rita's went from having no altar boys, to having three. I however, still held the distinction of being the very first altar boy, and remained the only one to be the continuous recipient of all those shiny quarters from Mr. Sensenbrenner.

I was so into the religious fervor that I decided I would become a priest when I grew up. I even went as far as setting up an altar in our living room (using my mom's ironing board) and practiced saying Mass (that is, until my mom caught me doing this and forbade me from continuing this ritual.)

Over the next three years, I would serve mass at two funerals, and also get to serve at St. Anne's with Fr. James Gutzler, who had presided at my First Communion Mass in 1956. It was also at St.

Anne's that I met my first Bishop, and I remember how deeply moving it was to be in the presence of someone so high in the church. We all felt it was an honor to kiss his ring. (Apparently they had a similar gesture of reverence and humility in La Cosa Nostra, but I didn't find that out until I read "*The Godfather*", many years later....)

Lest you get the impression that I was a very pious and well behaved boy in my youth, what I will tell you next will dispel all that. Let's look in on two pint-sized protesters, and their unique method of demonstrating their displeasure over that whole Winegar to Presque Isle name change affair....

The Great Paper Protest

Hands on his hips, Tom asked "What in the holy hell are you two little buttholes doing?"

As you may recall from an earlier chapter, the town started out in 1905 as Fosterville, and in 1910 was changed to Winegar, when William S. Winegar bought the mill, and that name remained until 1955. Because the mill and Mr. Winegar were both long gone, the residents of the town voted to change the name once again. Now the town would officially be known as "Presque Isle" which apparently is a French term meaning "almost an island" Everybody seemed to take the name change in stride; except that is, for Pat Finnegan and I.

Although the exact reason for our discontent remains somewhat unclear, our reaction to the name change is still vivid in my memory bank. Perhaps it was that the new name was too long, or that it sounded strange to us (even though the Presque Isle River flowed along right beside the town), or maybe we were just set in our ways and didn't like change, which would be somewhat unusual since I was only five years old and Pat was six at the time. Whatever the reason, we were determined to demonstrate our discontent for the whole town to see.

One quiet, overcast, Sunday morning, we put our plan into action. We had 'obtained'(and by 'obtained' I mean stolen) a stack of newspapers that Clarence Childers had put out by the side of the Red & White store for disposal. Carrying our load of newsprint, we walked down the hill a bit, until we were across from Novak's Hardware, where Main St. intersects with Church St.

The Red and White Store, located at the north end of Main St. in Winegar/Presque Isle. Photo courtesy of Mr. Jack Winegar

Setting down our bundle, we launched the "Great Paper Protest!" Each of us grabbed a sheet of paper and tore it into strips which we then threw out into the middle of the street. Our goal, I guess, was to completely cover the intersection with torn up newspaper; although, thinking back, I have absolutely no clue as to what we thought this would accomplish. But we excitedly tore that pile of paper into pieces and threw them into the air, spreading them left and right on the street, all the while laughing and just having a grand ol' time. We were also venting our anger at the Town Chairman, Mr. Fred Wolter, whom we held responsible for changing the name of our beloved Winegar. Our irritation with Mr. Wolter was misplaced though, as we later learned he had nothing to do with the re-naming of the town. But what did we know; after all we were only five and six years old....

We had been at our protest for about 15 minutes and, in my estimation, it was going well. We had about half the paper gone and the intersection was littered with newspaper strips. Our protest would be visible to anyone who came by!

Speaking of which, at that moment, someone did come by, namely Pat's older brother, Tom Finnegan. He came up the hill from their house on Church St. and looked at what we had done. Hands on his hips he asked "What in the holy hell are you two little buttholes doing?"

"We are protesting!" we announced in unison.

"Protesting what?"

"Changing the town name!" I responded.

"You are both idiots." Tom declared, "But I'll tell you what- you two dimwits better pick up all this paper before someone sees it, or someone's going to get a lickin' from Dad!"

It was right then that we realized that this protest might not have the results that we anticipated. It was quite possible that the residents of Presque Isle (fka Winegar) would not take kindly to our mass littering. Since it was a small town, word of this ill-intentioned stunt would no doubt get back to our parents and, if cousin Tom had anything to do with it, soon.

"OK! OK!" Pat pleaded. "Don't tell Dad! We'll pick it up!"

Not wanting be have our bottoms warmed by our fathers, Pat and I hurriedly started gathering up the strips of paper and crushing them together in balls, which we placed by the side of the road. One thing that we both found out was that we had indeed tore up a lot of newspaper! And all that paper was now drifting back and forth in the slight breeze, in the middle of Main St.

We scrambled to pick up all the paper that we could, but it was everywhere! Tom just stood by and watched with a smirk, as we struggled to hide the evidence of our crime, which could earn us both a trip to the woodshed.

As we went about our task, a car came up the hill from the south end of town. We didn't recognize the car or the driver, which was lucky I guess. It must have been someone passing thru town on their way to the U.P. But what we did notice was that, as the car passed by, the wind it created blew some of the newspaper strips off to the sides of the road. Hmmmmm…if a car could do that, why couldn't we? I quickly explained my plan to Pat, and in seconds we were both running back and forth through the field of paper strips, trying to create enough wind to blow them off the street.

The difference though, between us and the car of course, was the weight, the bulk, and the speed. The car was quite large, as most cars were in those days, weighed about 2,000 lbs, and was probably going at least 20 mph as it made its way past us. We had none of those things. We were two small boys, whose combined weight was under 110 lbs, and our top speed was probably a pathetic five mph. Suffice it to say, we failed miserably in our efforts to clear the debris from Main St.

Tom, however, thought our actions were hilarious, and he was practically beside himself with laughter. Hands clutching his sides, tears rolling down his cheeks, it was all he could do to keep from falling on the ground in hysterics. Finally, winded and wore out, Pat and I admitted defeat, and went slowly back to picking up the paper, one piece at a time.

It was at this point, that Tom came to our rescue. He jumped in and started grabbing strips of newspaper like a madman, crumpling them up, dropping them in the grass by the side of the street, and hustling back to pick up more. It took a while, but we soon had the street almost cleared. Fortunately, the wind came up, and scattered the few remaining strips in all directions.

We grabbed the balls of crumpled up paper and hid them in the pine trees that grew at the back of the school lot. After a few weeks and a couple of good rains, the evidence of our failed protest was gone, and our butts were saved, for the time being at least. Over the years we found other opportunities to get into mischief and since it was Presque Isle, a very small town where everybody knew everybody, we usually got caught and paid the price.

Mouse in the House

My mother was raised in the Catholic religion, and was not a woman given to objectionable language, however, I can tell you that, on that day, at that moment, she let out a stream of curse words that would have made a sailor blush....

We didn't have a lot of money, and I am sure that my parents survived paycheck to paycheck. However, we always had a roof over our heads, good food, clean clothes, and love. We also had our share of belly laughs....

One such laugh involved a twenty-pound bag of flour, my parents, a mouse, and a broom. Here is what happened:

Flour bags, sugar bags, and I am sure other bags as well at that time, came with a draw string at the top. When you wanted to open the bag for the first time, you pulled the drawstring that was threaded through the top edge of the bag until it opened enough to be able to reach in with a measuring cup and scoop out the flour. Of course, after you did this, the drawstring still stayed attached to the bag. On larger bags this string might end up being 8-9 inches long, and would end up hanging down inside the bag (there is a reason that I am explaining this in such detail, as you will soon see)

My mother liked to bake cakes, pies, and even homemade bread, on occasion. One Saturday morning, she decided to make a fresh apple pie for the dinner dessert. She got out the apples, peeled them and assembled the rest of the ingredients. Taking a measuring cup, she dipped it into the flour bag.

Suddenly she let out a blood curdling scream, dropped the cup, and scrambled as far away from the flour bag as she could!

"What the hell is going on?" my dad yelled from the living room.

"BILL! BILL! COME HERE! THERE'S A MOUSE IN THE FLOUR BAG!! QUICK! KILL IT!" she screeched. My father, rushing to the defense and protection of the woman he loved and adored, ran to the corner of the kitchen and, grabbing a broom, approached the flour bag.

Raising the broom, he brought it down squarely on the bag, which by now had tipped over on its' side, due to my mom's frenzied extraction of her hand from the clutches of the, as of yet unseen, mouse.

Now, this twenty-pound flour bag was still about three quarters full when my father's assault began. As he rained blow after blow down on that bag, two things happened. First, the bag became flatter and flatter, which I'm sure was dad's intent, wanting to squash that mouse into a little mousy pancake, if you will. However well intended his actions were, the second thing that happened to the bag was not only unintended, but also quite hilarious. You see, the reason the flour bag got thinner and thinner with each wallop of the broom, was that the flour was being forced out of the open end of the bag, and eventually out of even more rips in the bag as Dad attacked with a ferocity I rarely saw in him.

Not only was the flour forced out of the bag, it erupted into huge flour clouds that soon seemed to engulf every surface of our kitchen; the table, the chairs, the sink, refrigerator, stove and the floor. Everything that could have a white floury coating now did so. By the way, this coating also included both of my parents, who now appeared to be very, very, pale characters from a B grade "Walking Dead" movie. (Even though my mother's hair was brown until the day she died at age sixty, on that day, in that kitchen, we got a glimpse of what she might have looked like in her later years)

After beating the bag, and presumably the mouse inside it, into submission, my Dad, by now slightly winded from the exertion of saving his family from this ferocious flour eating rodent, dropped the broom and declared "He must be dead!"

Since, during the entire episode, none of us had observed the mouse exiting the bag and, since there were no rodent tracks on the flour covered floor of the room, it was a pretty safe bet the IF the mouse was in the bag then, as the coroner in the "Wizard of Oz" once declared "She's not only merely dead; she's really most sincerely dead!"

The next job for our fearless father, our hero, and family guardian, was the removal, and disposal of the aforementioned mouse. Reaching his very white hand into the bag, Dad began to feel around for the mouse carcass. He got a somewhat confused look on his face, but then turned to mom and asked "How did you know there was a mouse in this bag?"

"Because when I reached in, I felt its' tail" She replied,

Dad gave her an evil grin. "You felt his tail? You mean this tail?" he said as he pulled his hand out of the bag holding the (wait for it….wait for it….) DRAWSTRING!

"OH MY GOD!" Mom exclaimed. "Was that what I felt"

Dad stood up, holding the bag by the offending drawstring/mouse tail, and looked around the white coated kitchen, his flour covered wife, and partially flour covered children who had been watching from the kitchen door, and who had escaped most of the flour cloud.

"Yes dear," he snickered, "This is what you felt!"

He couldn't contain himself any longer as he looked at the flour devastation that had been caused by mom's mouse-guided mistake. He broke out into gales of laughter, dropping the bag, and clutching his sides. He was quickly joined by my mother, my sisters, and I, as we all laughed somewhat hysterically at what we had just witnessed.

With all of us pitching in, we eventually got the mess cleaned up, everyone got washed up and into flour free clothing, and we all piled in the car to have dinner at the Lure. Needless to say, none of us ordered any apple pie for dessert....

One of the other extremely entertaining events occurred in our backyard, the following spring. My Dad and my uncle, Jack Finnegan, both owned motor boats that they kept docked on Little Horsehead Lake, just over the hill from our house. They had a great time with those boats, and it was always a treat for us when we got to go out on the lake with them. I do remember that the very first time Uncle Jack let my cousin Pat drive his boat, Pat came about six inches away from slamming into the dock as he took off. Uncle Jack didn't let him drive the boat again for the rest of the summer.

That spring Dad had pulled his 15 horsepower Evinrude motor out of the boat and attached it to a 50 gallon barrel, filled with water, in our back yard. As he was tuning up the motor and had it idling in the barrel, Mom came out, and was watching dad work. She saw a small stream of water spraying out of the back of the motor (this was from the pee hole tube, which is an indicator that water is flowing thru the motor, something which is pretty darn important).

Not being at all familiar with the workings of an outboard motor, she innocently asked my father, "Why is the water squirting out of that hole?"

Dad leaned over and looked at the back of the motor and said "Hmmm… I don't know. Keep a close eye on it for a second while I try something."

Mom bent over for a closer look at the water stream, while Dad, with a mischievous smirk on his face, returned to the front of the motor and grabbed the throttle lever. "Are you watching it?" he asked Mom.

"Oh yeah", she replied, leaning in even closer to the edge of the barrel.

"OK, keep watching and let me know what you see."

With that my father stepped as far away from the barrel as he could, while still being able to reach the motor control. He cast one more look at Mom, then twisted that throttle control to full open! It must have taken all of about .0000002 seconds for 50 gallons of water to shoot straight up out of the barrel, and descend on my poor unsuspecting mother, drenching her from head to foot! She shrieked and jumped back from the barrel, screaming at my Dad who, even though he had not completely escaped the waterfall, was not nearly as wet as Mom. He immediately shut the motor off and, barely able to control himself, asked "What did you see?"

Now, my mother was raised in the Catholic religion, and was not a woman given to objectionable language, but I can tell you that, on that day, at that moment, she let out a stream of curse words that would have made a sailor blush. My father was somewhat oblivious to this verbal assault, as he was just about rolling on the ground in a fit of hysterical laughter.

My mother spotted the garden hose laying by the side of the barrel, picked it up and, opening the nozzle full blast, proceeded to spray Dad, who was trying frantically to escape. In a few seconds he was as drenched as Mom, and she threw down the hose.

"There, Mr. Smart Ass! How do you like it?" she hollered. They stood there looking at each other for a moment, then both broke out into a laughing fit, stumbling around the yard, laughing until tears ran down their faces, and blended in with their soaked clothes. When they finally got control of themselves, they hugged, kissed, and went in to change into dry clothes. But my mom never asked Dad any mechanical questions ever again....

A Visit from "Da Bears"

"I caught up with one of the cubs and I grabbed him. I had him by both ears. As long as you hang onto them like that they won't fight you that hard."

-Chet Dumask

In between Lake St, and McKenzie Pl, just to the east of Glenn Fairfield's house, was a small grove of trees. For some unknown reason, one September night, a female black bear and her two cubs wandered into town and took up residence in the grove. As you can imagine this was quite a dangerous situation, and it needed to be handled immediately. What happened next caused quite a bit of controversy in our little town. I'll let Chet Dumask, one of the main participants in this event, tell the story, in his own words:

"My dog, Duke, broke off his leash one night, and was down by the streetlight by the Reitzloff house. I called for him, but he wouldn't come when I called him. He just stood there looking at me. I said "C'mon Duke, c'mon home" but he just stood there. All of a sudden I see a cub bear go over the road toward Little Horsehead Lake. And that was probably the same cub bear that I ended up catching in my hands, because he was going over the same spot, a couple of days later.

"In the morning, Duke was down there barking again. There was one willow tree in that grove that was leaning way down. Up in the tree was a big 'ol bear. Well, Duke starts going up on that willow tree barking at the bear. I'm yelling for Duke to come to me, because the bear is now starting to back down from the tree. You see, they won't come down forwards, they will always climb down backwards. So I took Duke home, and locked him up and I told my wife to call Ben Bendrick, the game warden, and tell him there was a big bear here with a couple of cubs and what did he want us to do? I got my rifle, and went down and shot the big bear, before she could attack anyone.

"Big John Eschenbauch came over with his bow, and he told me "Why don't you go get your bow, Chet? Because if they say we can shoot 'em, we'll shoot 'em.

"I got my bow, and then the town constable came over to us and said "If there is anyone here with a bow license, it is strictly legal to shoot the bears". Big John says "Well Chet, you saw them first, so you go ahead and shoot first." I picked out the biggest cub, and by that time there was a pretty good crowd coming around. So I shot the cub, and it fell from the tree and hit the ground, crying. You know, when they cry they sound like a human. So Big John shot at his, a couple of times but he only wounded it. One of his arrows ended up in the roof of his mother's house a few hundred feet away.

"In the crowd there was some guys there; I think they were from Ohio. They said they were bear hunters, and they had a real thick rope with them. Now, why they needed a rope that thick, I surely don't know.

"After John's bear was wounded it came down from the tree. And it took off toward the lake, just like the one did the other night. So, I saw where it was headed and I run like hell, and when I caught up to him I grabbed him. I had him by both ears. As long as you hang onto them like that they won't fight you that hard. Of course he was squirming quite a bit and then my hands was getting a little tired. I got him about halfway back to the tree where he had been, and here these guys come with that great big rope and one of them said "Here, put this rope around his neck and we'll shoot him!" I said "No, no, I'm not going to do that' One of the others said "I'll do it. I'll tie it on there!" I told them "OK, go ahead; he's all yours"

"So he ropes the bear and is holding one end of the rope while the bear is bouncing up and down trying to get away. His buddy is shooting at it, and he had to shoot about three times to kill it. And of course all those people seen that, and a lot of them were pretty upset, and they were pointing fingers at me.

"Later on somebody complained to Ben Bendrick "What was the deal down there with that guy shootin' all them bear? That Chet Dumask, guy?" Bendrick told him "Anytime a bear comes to town with her cubs and stays 2-3 days, it is very dangerous. Chet Dumask did this town a favor.

"A few days later Stella McKenzie had a big bear trying to break into her place. Mae Prosser called me and said that Stella wanted me to come up and shoot the bear. I agreed to go, but told both of them keep quiet and not mention me, because there was still a lot of rabble rousing going on about the bear cubs we killed.

"I took my rifle and went up to Stella's house and killed the bear. I told her to call Bendrick and tell him that a bear had been trying to break into her house, as evidenced by the broken screen door, and that someone had shot it, but she didn't know who. Well, Bendrick knew it was me that killed it, but he never said a word.

"I know there were people that were upset about what we had done, but we had no choice but to kill the bears, so we did what we had to do"

If bears come into the town, or are threatening nearby property, then they had to be dealt with. It was a little different a few miles to the west of town, at the town dump. Each night in the summer, bears would come out of the woods from behind the dump, and forage thru the garbage for food. This was pretty exciting for the tourists, as they don't get to see these animals in Milwaukee or Chicago.

Bear watching at the dump became a popular summer evening pastime. Some nights there might be 15-20 cars full of families parked on the circular access road to the dump pit. This activity became such a big event, that the town decided to actually promote it. Instead of being referred to as the "town dump", they erected a sign at the entrance on Highway W, that proudly proclaimed that the site was now known as the "Presque Isle Bear Pit". This attracted even more tourists, and some nights there were so many cars up there, that the locals had to start dropping off their trash much earlier in the day, to avoid the crowds.

It was alright to drive in, and watch the bears from the safety of your car, but every once in a while there would be someone who wanted a better picture, so they would step out of their vehicles, and that was a recipe for trouble. My family was at the Bear Pit one evening, and my father had brought along his Kodak 8mm movie camera. He was taking movies of a bear, from the car, which was the safe and sane way to do that. At one point the bear decided that he was no longer hungry and started ambling back toward the forest. My dad however, apparently did not think he had filmed enough of the action. Against our protests, he jumped from the car and began running after this huge black bear. Fortunately for him, the bear was somewhat intimidated by this crazy man chasing him, and picked up his pace considerably, quickly disappearing into the woods. At this point, my father came to his senses, and decided that going into the woods, at night, and following a beast as big and powerful as Smokey's cousin, would not be the best choice he could make. We all breathed a collective sigh of relief, as dad gave up the chase and returned to the car. All the way home, my mother made sure that he understood that, in her opinion, what had just transpired was not only dangerous, but showed a complete lack of functioning brain cells, on his part. Her message must have gotten thru, because I don't recall him ever doing that again.

Bob Hill tells of the fun he had one night at the Bear Pit:

"As a kid we were up there, and there's a guy who came up to the Pit to take pictures. Well, this bear starts coming at him, and he's backin' up with his camera. He gets by my car and as a prank, I just reached out and grabbed him by the ass, and yelled "AAARRGGHHH!!!!" I don't know what he got pictures of but, the next thing we knew, he was on the hood of the car kickin' and scratchin' and screamin'! Everybody thought I was an asshole, except me. But, you know, it just seemed like the likely thing to do at the time. Actually I'd do it again today if the opportunity rolls this way and the same dumb bastard would try that again."

The bears weren't the only unwelcome visitors to come to town. Apparently a couple of wanted felons felt the need to escape to "Wisconsin's last Wilderness" as well....

Hot Pursuit

As they got to the open space, he stood up, pointed the Tommy gun at them and shouted "Stop where you are, or I'll cut 'ya in half!"

On July 24th, 1958, an intense manhunt for two gunmen who had escaped from a chase by Vilas and Oneida County police ended on the main street of Presque Isle.

The two men, John Chipman, age 27, and Ray Emery, age 26, were wanted for burglaries in Crandon and Milwaukee, and also for parole violations. Police estimated that they had committed some 200 break-ins. The men were considered to be 'armed and dangerous'.

As their descriptions were being broadcast to all law enforcement agencies in Vilas and Oneida counties, and even into the Upper Peninsula of Michigan, they somehow managed to avoid capture, at one point crashing through a roadblock north of Woodruff. Police shot at the car and gunfire was returned by the two desperate men, as they raced north on Highway 51, at speeds of 90-120 miles per hour. During the chase, gunfire from the fleeing car shattered the windshield of the pursuing Minocqua squad car, narrowly missing the officers inside. The officers lost the car near Hwy 51 and County

Road H, when apparently the gunmen turned off on one of several side roads in the area. Local police surrounded the area with roadblocks, but somehow the two men eluded them.

Chipman and Emery made their way up thru Boulder Junction. Not wanting to risk running into the police by staying on a main highway, they turned off just north of Boulder Junction, and traveled down an old logging road until their car became stuck in the sand. They abandoned it there, and hiked northwest through the dense woods, until they came to County Highway B, some six miles from where they had left their vehicle.

It was at that point that they made a crucial mistake, one that would lead to their ultimate demise. Had they crossed Highway B, and continued north thru the forest for just another two miles, they would have crossed the state line into Michigan, and quite possibly been able to escape apprehension by hiding out in one of the many cabins nestled deep in the pines. Instead, they walked west, along the highway, until they came to a private road, leading to the Anna Lake Resort home of John Auschen. Mr. Auschen was not home at the time, but his caretaker, John Eschenbauch, Sr. was there doing yard work.

Tired and thirsty from their overland trek, Chipman called out to Eschenbauch, "Hey! You got any water here?" Because Eschenbauch had been out of town all morning working, he knew nothing of the intense manhunt that was underway for these two men. So, he was just being hospitable when he replied "Yah, got plenty of water! Come in the house, and I'll get you some."

As they greedily drank the cold water, John asked them if they were hitch hiking. Exchanging glances with each other, Chipman, the apparent leader of the two, said "Yeah, we were fishing and got lost."

"Well, I'm going to be leaving in a bit and heading into Presque Isle." replied John, "I can give you a lift there if you want." The men readily accepted Eschenbauch's offer, and soon they piled into his car, and drove into town.

Reaching the center of our small hamlet, John Eschenbauch stopped his car outside Gunnar Larson's tavern. Chipman and Emery, by now feeling a bit more secure, since no one seemed to take notice of them, decided to stop in for a cold beer. They invited John Eschenbach to join them, and they headed into the bar. After buying Eschenbauch a beer for driving them to town, they downed a few more and began to relax. Emery mentioned that he was hungry, and they asked about getting some food. Gunnar told them to try The Lure, which was located two buildings north of the bar. They finished their beers, left three dollars on the bar, and walked to the restaurant.

There were however, two things that the men didn't know. First, although the town seemed to be nothing more than a sleepy, backward little village, almost everyone in Presque Isle knew about the manhunt, and that cops from all over the area, including the FBI, the Wisconsin State Patrol, and the Michigan State Police were quietly converging on the town.

Second, among the bar patrons at Gunnar's that day, was a vacationing policeman from Bayfield County, Sheriff Frank Utpadel, and his wife. While he did not have any weapons on his person, Utpadel did have a Thompson sub-machine gun in the trunk of his car out front. After the hungry crooks left the bar, he made his way outside and, donning a long coat that he kept in the back seat of his car, he retrieved the Tommy gun from the trunk and concealed it under the coat.

Looking south from the center of town. Just past The Lure, was the Red Owl store and Gunnar Larson's tavern, across from the Mobil station. It was between the two telephone poles where the Sheriff drew down on the wanted men. Photo courtesy of Brenda Dyre.

Meanwhile two Michigan State Police officers approached Chet Dumask and asked if he knew where the men had gotten picked up at? He had been out on a minnow run, and had seen them hiking on the road by Anna Lake Resort. The cops asked Chet to show them where he had seen them, so he got in their car and they took off out of town. Chet was not impressed with these officers and told me that "I got in their car, and I have to tell you that for a 'goldarn State cop, that guy couldn't drive for shit! I knew that if he was ever chasing me I wouldn't have to worry about getting away!"

While they were on their way out to investigate that, other cops were busy as well. The roads in and out of town were blocked, and now it was only a matter of time before they moved in on the criminals.

But back to Sheriff Utpadel, and his Tommy gun. He had instructed his wife to go to The Lure, and make sure the two were still there. While she was doing that, he positioned himself near the line of cars on the street and waited. Mrs. Utpadel got to the restaurant and went inside. While she was there, Emery and Chipman, still unaware of the net that was closing in on them, left the restaurant, and headed back towards Gunnar's. Mrs. Utpadel followed them out, but she turned north, safely away from the trouble that was about to take place.

For some reason, the men seemed now to be more suspicious of their surroundings, walking with their heads down, but still looking all around at the same time. As they made their way behind the parked cars, Sheriff Utpadel moved closer, keeping himself hidden from their view. (Remember that back then cars were built much bigger and higher than today's models, so it didn't take much ducking down for him to keep out of sight).

He had chosen his position well. The robbers had to cross an opening between two parked cars on their way to Gunnar's. Utpadel was waiting, and ready. As they got to the open space, he stood up, pointed the Tommy gun at them and shouted "Stop where you are, or I'll cut 'ya in half!" Chipman, knowing the jig was up, shouted back "You wouldn't talk so big if you didn't have that Tommy gun!"

"Maybe so", Utpadel replied, "But I do have the gun, so get your damn hands in the air, NOW!"

As the two felons reached for the sky, it seemed like every squad car from the entire state closed in on the scene. To add to the excitement, now everyone in town was pouring out of their houses to see what was happening. At the center of it all, in the middle of Main street, stood Sheriff Frank Utpadel, calmly holding his trusty Tommy gun, while thirty feet in front of him, stood two very unhappy desperados.

(A little side note here. Seated in one of the parked cars that the crooks walked past, was Roy Hartmann's wife, Doris. Ray Emery turned to her and said "Hi beautiful!" before continuing on. Told of this remark, Roy Hartmann later said, laughingly, "Boy, those guys WERE crazy!" I am sure Doris did not find that remark very funny.)

Other policemen exited their cars and, with their own guns drawn, quickly handcuffed the two, and placed them each in separate squads. I think everyone breathed a sigh of relief that things hadn't degenerated into a shoot-out at high noon on Main Street. And it could have, since Chipman did have a pistol in the waistband of his pants. But he had been so surprised by the Bayfield cop pointing a Tommy gun at him and his partner in crime, that he knew if he had pulled out his gun, he would quite literally have been "cut in half" as Frank Utpadel had promised.

For my part, I do remember walking up to the side of the squad car and looking in. It was the first time I have ever seen an actual criminal up close, and I wasn't about to miss out on the opportunity. It was Ray Emery and he was kind of disappointing to look at; short, ugly, and not real mean looking at all. He was nothing at all like the bad guys I saw on TV. I looked at him and smirked. He turned toward me, and sneered. "Get away from me, you little bastard!" I backed up pretty quick, I'll tell you that! I was sure glad he was in handcuffs and that there was a whole bunch of cops around!

Soon the squad cars containing the captured fugitives headed out of town, and the rest of us gathered around Sheriff Utpadel in admiration. Men were slapping him on the back and offering to buy him and his wife drinks, dinner and whatever else they could think of to reward him for his bravery for the apprehension of the crooks. My cousins, Pat and Tom Finnegan, and I really wanted to get a closer look at the Thompson sub-machine gun, but unfortunately, it was now once again resting in the trunk of the Sheriff's personal car. While I would see lots of machine guns later on "The Untouchables" TV show in a few years, this was the first time any of us boys had ever seen a real Tommy gun though, and we were all excited about it.

While the excitement slowly died down, the story of the two robbers, dominated the conversations in town for days.

John Chipman and Ray Emery were eventually tried and convicted of numerous charges and sent off to the state prison in Waupun to serve their sentences. I am quite sure that if they ever did get out of prison, neither of them ever again thought that a trip to the Northwoods would be a good idea....

If you can get sent to the "Big House" for burglary and violating your parole, what do you think the sentence would be for smoking and setting the house on fire? Let's find out....

"Uh, Dad...
The House is on Fire!"

"On a scale of 1 to 10, that spanking probably rated at least a 9.5, as far as we could determine from all the yelling, crying, and smacking sounds coming from the other side of the bedroom door."

My sister Sherry is five years older than me; Cindy is three years older. Sherry had just started smoking at age 14, and was doing pretty well at hiding her new found vice from my parents. I guess that, since both my mom and dad were smokers, they did not catch on to the smell of tobacco on her or her clothes. Other kids her age were also into the habit, and although I did not know where or how they got the cigarettes, it must not have been too hard, since Sherry always seemed to have a pack in her purse.

Of course, as the little brother, it was my sworn duty to blackmail her at every opportunity. All I had to do was hint that I would tell our parents about the pack of Lucky Strikes she had, and she would either cough up some money for ice cream and comic books, or she would end up doing some of my chores for me. Ahhh, life was good!

At the time we were living in the house by St. Rita's. Dad had bought this house from my uncle, Jack Finnegan. The house consisted of a kitchen, living room, and two bedrooms, so I shared the front bedroom with my sisters. When my cousins, Tom and Pat Finnegan lived there, they also shared that room.

The walls of the house were made from plaster and lathe and covered with wallpaper, which was common at the time. In this particular room, there was a hole in the plaster about three feet above the floor. This hole measured approximately four inches long and three inches wide. It was down this hole that Tom, Pat, my sisters, and I, occasionally dropped pieces of paper and other objects.

View from the south end of Main St. at the dam on Little Horsehead Lake circa 1956. In the distance you can see the white house where my family lived, and next to it, St. Rita's Catholic Church. Photo courtesy of Ms. Brenda Dyre.

My parents had left the house to buy groceries, and Sherry decided to light up. My curiosity got the better of me, and I decided I wanted to see what this smoking was all about. I demanded that she give me one of her cigarettes. She initially refused, but under threat of me exposing her secret, she reluctantly lit a cigarette and handed it to me. My other sister, Cindy, also got in the act and soon we all were puffing away. I was not doing as well as the girls since I had never tried this before, and after my first couple of puffs, I was rethinking my desire for this habit. It was at this moment, that we heard my dad's car pull up in our gravel driveway. Sherry and Cindy quickly tossed their cigarettes out the bedroom window, but I, now in full panic mode, did not follow suit. Nope, I made the disastrous and fateful decision to throw my lit cigarette down the hole in the bedroom wall! (I can honestly say that this was one of the least intelligent decisions I have ever made in my life, although, as you will soon see, it had much worse consequences for my sister than it did for me...)

About five minutes went by, and my sisters and I noticed that small tendrils of smoke were wafting out of the aforementioned hole. Apparently some of the accumulated refuse residing between the walls had been ignited. This was definitely a problem, but one I thought I could solve. All I needed to do was douse the fire and our secret would remain undiscovered.

So, off to the kitchen I went. Unfortunately, both of my parents were also in the kitchen; mom enjoying a cup of coffee, and dad with a cold beer. As casually as possible, I went to the sink and filled an empty Mason jar with cold water. As I turned back, my dad said, "Where are you going with that?"

"Sherry's thirsty." I responded and quickly headed back to the bedroom, where I emptied the jar of water down the smoking hole. "Whew!" I whispered to my sisters, "That was close!"

Unfortunately, my relief was short lived as, a few minutes later, smoke was once again rising out of that darn opening; And, it was coming out even heavier than before. Still, I thought I could save the day, and our butts, so I grabbed the Mason jar and headed back to the kitchen, where I once again filled it to the brim and tried to make a quick exit.

"Where in the heck are you going with all that water?" my dad asked.

"Uh, Sherry is still thirsty!" I practically yelled, as I ran from the room.

My second attempt to extinguish the burning garbage between the walls of the bedroom was just as unsuccessful as my first attempt. After a minute or two, we all knew that the fire was beyond our control. Since I was the one who had put the lit cigarette down the hole in the first place, my sisters decided that I should be the one to tell our mom and dad what was going on. As I slowly made my way to the kitchen to break the news that our house may be destroyed, I came up with the only thing that I thought could save myself from having to stand up while eating supper for the next few days.

Reaching the kitchen, I went to my dad and said, "Daddy, if you promise not to hit me, I'll tell you something."

Smiling, he replied, "Well, OK, I promise. What is it?"

"THE HOUSE IS ON FIRE!" I cried, pointing toward the bedroom. Both my parents rushed to the front of the house, where the smoke was still pouring out of that cursed hollow. (At least my dumping the two jars of water has slowed the spread of the flames a little).

Dad ran to the shed and grabbed his axe. Returning, he proceeded to chop a hole in the wall of that bedroom that was about four feet high and a foot wide. In the meantime, mom had filled a bucket of water and stood by ready to pour. Between them, they were able to quash the flames. Although there was plaster, lathe, soggy paper and water all over the floor, at least our house was saved from becoming a pile of charred rubble.

Now that the fire was out, the investigation into its origin, and the interrogation of those involved (meaning my sisters and myself) began. During the course of my particular questioning, while I did admit to throwing a lit cigarette down the hole, not only was I able to shift the blame for this whole incident onto my sister, Sherry, but I was able to remind my father of the promise he made not to strike me, his only son, his pride and joy, the innocent victim of his sister's nasty and disgusting smoking habit. (Yes, even at that age I did have the ability to sometimes talk my way out of suffering the consequences of bad behavior).

To my father's credit, and my great relief, he kept his promise that day, and I was spared the punishment that I actually so richly deserved. Sherry, on the other hand was not so lucky in that regard. Back then, even if you were in your teens, you were not too old to spanked and, in this particular instance, Sherry was the receiving end of my dad's leather belt. Cindy and I were sent from the room, and we listened as my oldest sister cried and begged for mercy, all to no avail. On a scale of 1 to 10, this spanking probably rated at least a

9.5, as far as we could determine from all the yelling, crying, and smacking sounds coming from the other side of the bedroom door.

When Dad was done administering Sherry's punishment, he proceeded to warn both Cindy and myself what would happen to us if we ever got caught with a cigarette again. With him waving the belt in our faces, and the sounds of Sherry still blubbering quite loudly from the bedroom, we were quick to give our solemn promises that we would never, ever, touch tobacco again as long as we lived.

Eventually, Sherry quieted down and, although I am sure she was very uncomfortable sitting for a few days, she managed to make a full recovery. She spent a lot of that time shooting me dirty looks which indicated that, if she thought she could get away with it, she would have no problem dismembering me and disposing of my body in the town dump. Of course, having been spared from suffering the same painful punishment that she had endured, due to my quick thinking and deal making with dad, I delighted in giving her lots of smirks, and I occasionally patted myself on the butt and laughed at her discomfort. Why, you ask, would I act this way? Because that's what little brothers do.....

Unfortunately, a few years later, our house did catch fire (through no fault of yours truly) and suffered extensive damage. We were lucky that the Presque Isle Volunteer Fire Department was able to respond and save our home from being completely destroyed. For that, we must say "Thank You Fred Wolter!"

Fred Wolter Changes the Town

"I loved that not only did I get a chance to live and grow here, but that I was able to make a living for my family here."

-Carl Wolter

Mr. Fred Wolter started the Winegar Volunteer Fire Department in 1949, when he purchased a civil defense pumper truck, equipped it with fire-fighting equipment, and convinced some of the men in town to be part of the department. Frank Jirikowic, Bill Hill, Hank Brousil, Deke Wilutis, and others, volunteered. Now the town had a chance to possibly save some buildings, instead of just standing by and watching them burn to the ground.

The town was divided regarding Mr. Wolter. When he first came here they were going to run him out of town, partly because of his German heritage. He came to town, bought land and then would not let people come on his property. He told them "I bought this land and I own it. You are not coming on my land". Before he bought the land everyone pretty much had the run of the entire township, and they could hunt, fish, and trap wherever they wanted to. He changed that, and the men of the town were not happy. Their feelings were that many of them had fought in WWII and there was no way some German guy was going to deprive them of their lifestyle.

Fred ran for Town Chairman and lost. Undeterred, he waited until the next election, ran for office again, and this time he won by a narrow margin. He then remained in office for the next twelve years, partly due to the efficiency of the town board, but also due to his ability to win over the opposition. During this period many significant improvements were made to both the village and the entire township.

According to his son, Carl, who later had his own time as Town Chairman, his father's biggest accomplishment in office took place in 1956, when he spearheaded the passing of zoning ordinances regarding waterfront development, requiring all newly divided lakefront lots be at least 1.5 acres, and have a minimum of 200 feet of frontage. This ordinance was the first of its' kind in Vilas County, and was soon adopted by other communities throughout the county and the state. Due to Fred's vision and leadership, Presque Isle has continued to provide residents and visitors the peace and quiet that can still be found in the natural environment of "Wisconsin's Last Wilderness".

In addition, Fred is credited with cleaning up waste and mismanagement in the town government. He put an end to some of the practices of misuse of town funds for personal use, and restored fiscal responsibility to the community.

Under his watch, the quality of the town roads was greatly improved. He was not only able to obtain better equipment, but led the effort to construct a new municipal garage to house and maintain the trucks, graders, plows and other equipment that was required to care for the infrastructure of the township.

At the end of his tenure he was succeeded in office by a new town chairman, but Fred was not happy with the way things were being done, and was considering running again in 1964. Unfortunately, on January 29th, 1964, while trying to skid a fallen pine tree across the ice on one of the lakes on his property, his tractor broke through the ice, and Fred drowned.

Today, the Wolter family's legacy lives on, in the Catherine Wolter Wilderness Area. This 3,000 acre nature preserve includes 15 lakes and ponds with 36,000 feet of undeveloped shoreline. The wilderness area is an undisturbed gem in the heart of Presque Isle and will allow the enjoyment of nature in its most pristine state for years to come. It is open to the public from sunrise to sunset for hiking, cross country skiing, snowshoeing, bird-watching and other low impact recreational activities, and I would strongly suggest that you take to time to visit this wonderful area. Fred and Catherine would be very proud that their three children pushed for the creation of this wilderness area, rather than have it developed, and they have this as their legacy.

Tragically, Fred was not the only resident of the town to die in the waters of our many lakes. Which is why, every fall, the following warning was given....

Don't Go Near the Water!

"You just trot off to your room and get out of those wet clothes. I'll be there in a few minutes, and we will 'discuss' why you were down by that lake when you were told not to go there."

-My mother

"DO NOT GO ON THE ICE UNTIL I TELL YOU IT IS SAFE!"

Each year, as the weather changed from fall to winter, and the lakes began to freeze over, this was the stern warning given to every child in town by their parents. It was usually followed by a very brief reason for the warning- "A boy drowned out there because he went on the ice too early- so STAY OFF THE LAKE!" We were never given any of the details of this tragic incident, and I guess we, or at least I, didn't press my parents about it. It was sufficient that the warning had been given, received, and understood.

Robert Lahaie was seven years old when he drowned in Little Horsehead Lake on December 1, 1951. He was the son of Gladys Shaddock, and the grandson of Maytha Shaddock. Years later, I would ask Chet Dumask to fill me in on what had actually happened to the boy:

"His mother heard him singing a song "I sail my ship alone", as he walked out to the ice. And then all of a sudden he went in. I don't know where I was when I heard her screaming, but someone yelled "Bobby fell in! Bobby fell in!" I ran down off the hill by the house they lived in. He was laying on the bottom just like Glenn Fairfield was when I pulled him out. He drowned in Big Horsehead. They were both laying on the bottom, arms and legs outstretched, face down."

Postcard showing aerial view of Presque Isle, circa 1960's.
Photo courtesy of Ms. Brenda Dyre

Glenn Fairfield drowned in Big Horsehead Lake on November 11, 1958. Once again, Chet was the man on the scene:

"There was no ice on the lake yet. He was out by the rushes, fishing for perch. I was out mink trackin' as it was the fall of the year. I came by there and out comes Vern Aikens, and he is all soaking wet up to his chest. He told me "Glenn drowned out there! He tipped over in his canoe; he was fishing. And he was hollering, "HELP!" But he's only got that one hand he can hang on with, cuz' the other one was off. And I don't see him anymore; he must have drowned!"

"I said, "OK. I'll run home and get my little pram boat. I raced home, got the little pram, and loaded it into the back of my Jeep CJ. I zipped back out to the lake, and I rowed out to where Glenn had gone under. There he was, on the bottom; face down, legs and arms out."

Of course, not knowing what had actually happened to Bobby Lahaie, the parental warnings seemed to be a bit overly cautious. Sometimes, as a boy, even though you know the danger, hear the warnings, and know the consequences to be paid for not heeding said warnings, you push the limits anyway.

Now, going out onto the ice before it is safe can only result in one of three things happening. 1) The ice holds your weight, you play on the lake for a while, nothing happens, and your parents do not find out. 2) The ice breaks and you fall in, but it is shallow enough that you are able to get out. Unfortunately, even though you are not dead, you are soaking wet and freezing, or 3) The ice breaks, you fall in the lake and drown, and your story becomes the subject of future warnings from the parents of the town, and chapters written in books into the next century. Trust me on this- when you venture out onto untested ice, one of those three things will happen to you. How do I know this, you ask? Let me relate to you my personal experience in this area.

Since our house was directly across the street and up the hill from Little Horsehead Lake, I spent a lot of time there. One cloudy

November day, when I was about nine years old, I was standing on the dock, where my Dad kept his boat tied up in the summer. Pat and Tom Finnegan were with me. It had been cold for the last couple of days, and a sheet of ice had formed over most of the lake, leaving an area of open water about 100 feet from the shore.

As we stood on the dock looking at the THIN sheet of BLACK ice that surrounded the pier, I could not help myself from reaching out with my foot and tapping the ice. Did I forget to mention that the wooden pier was covered with frost? Frost that can make footing somewhat slippery? Well, it was, and it did. As I tapped my right foot on the ice, my left foot suddenly decided that it no longer wanted to be on the dock, and instead wanted to join its twin on the ice. While the ice was firm enough to hold up to some gentle foot tapping, it was not nearly thick enough to support my weight, even though I probably only weighed 60 pounds soaking wet which, by the way, is exactly what I became a few seconds later.

As I heard and felt the ice give way, one thought flashed thru my mind; I was dead! Either I would die in the icy waters of Little Horsehead or, if I survived that fate, my mother was surely going to kill me herself when she found out what I had been up to. Fortunately, the first scenario did not play out, as I only sunk down waist deep in the frigid water. Tom and Pat immediately reached over and pulled me back up onto the dock. So, I was going to live, at least for a little while.

My next problem that had to be dealt with was getting home and getting into dry clothes without being caught by mom. In this, I would not be as lucky as I had been in surviving my plunge into the lake. We made it up the hill to my house, and my cousins suddenly decided that they needed to be somewhere else- anywhere else, but with me. Off they went, wishing me good luck, and laughing as they left. I now had no choice but to go in and face the music. In order to get to my bedroom, I had to go in the back door of the house, and cross the kitchen safely without arousing attention. Unfortunately for me, my mom was sitting at the kitchen table drinking coffee and visiting with my aunt, Delcie Dean, from Marenisco.

I opened the door, and tried to make a mad dash for my room, but something caught the attention of the two women. I think it may have been the loud squishing sounds my shoes were making, or perhaps it was the trail of water I was leaving on the linoleum floor. Whichever one it was, I was busted!

"What the h---?" my mother exclaimed as she took in the sight of her son, dripping wet, pants soaked, and shoes oozing water at every step. It took her about two seconds to completely ascertain why I was in such condition.

"YOU WERE IN THE LAKE, WEREN'T YOU?" she yelled. I knew by the tone and volume of her question, that I would probably have been much better off had I actually been in the lake right then, instead of here.

Knowing that there was no other plausible explanation for my watery situation, I was forced to tell the truth, and admit that I had indeed just come from the aforementioned lake. You know the old saying "The truth can set you free"? I suppose it can, but it can also lead to a very painful future. Trying to minimize the severity of the danger, and also my upcoming punishment, I attempted an explanation,

"I-I was just on the dock with Tom and Pat, and my foot slipped off, and I fell in the water, right by the dock, and it wasn't deep, and I got out right away, and I just need to change clothes, and I'll be ok, and…"

"Yes, you just trot off to your room and get out of those wet clothes," mom cut me off, with a somewhat suspicious hiss in her voice. "I'll be in in a few minutes, and we will 'discuss' why you were down by that lake when you were told not to go there."

As I headed off to my room, I heard my aunt telling mom that she really had to get going back home, and she could see that mom had "business to take care of". Aunt Delcie had no sooner left the house, when a very irate woman stormed into my room, waving her dreaded wooden hairbrush. I knew she wasn't there to work on the cowlick that I always sported, so I guessed correctly that the brush was to be used for another purpose.

"You went down by the lake, even after we have told you a thousand times not to, until we say it is safe, didn't you?" she said, as she sat on the bed and pulled me over her knee. Soon that hairbrush was smacking my bottom, and I was howling and promising I would never, ever go near the lake again.

I suppose that some of you may think this form of punishment was severe, and at the time, I would have certainly agreed with you. However, I learned two valuable lessons that day- 1) Black Ice Matters, and 2) a spanking trumps drowning any day…..

Fresh Bakery

"In the mornings you could smell the fragrance of fresh baked goods all over town."

As you entered Winegar from the south, and headed up Main Street, one of the first houses you saw was a very impressive green structure that sat on the right hand side of the street. This particular building was significant for two reasons. During the lumber era, this was the town home of William S. Winegar, whom the town was named after. Mr. Winegar also had a log cottage on Peaceful Island, in Oxbow Lake, just east of town.

When I lived in town, that house took on great importance every summer. The owners of the house, the Harnisch family, ran a bakery on Milwaukee's south side. During the summer months, members of the family came to Presque Isle and opened a bakery in that house, and what a bakery it was! In the mornings you could smell the fragrance of fresh baked goods all over town. Even though most of the women in town baked on a regular basis, the Harnisch family bakery did very well each summer.

Carl Wolter remembers that his parents, Fred and Catherine, would bring Carl and his sister Lorelei into town with them to buy bread from the bakery. Unfortunately, Mr. Wolter would put the bread in the back seat of the family car with the two children. As Carl remembers, there were more than a few times that half the bread was eaten by the time they arrived home.

One other reason that all of the kids in town could hardly wait for the Harnisch family to arrive each summer, was the raft. The yard on the backside of the bakery sloped down to the shore of Little Horsehead Lake. This particular part of the lake was basically the town swimming hole, and when the Harnisch's would get to town, one of the first things they did was put the red and white swimming raft out in the center of the bay. There it would stay until they left shortly before Labor Day. I think, at one time or another, every kid who lived in town swam out to that raft. Those were really some great times, and we really appreciated the Harnisch's for their generosity.

Kathleen Reitzloff Newberry remembers the bakery – "I remember that when our family came to Presque Isle, we arrived in the middle of the night. Next morning daddy went to the bakery and bought a bunch of bakery which we never got when living in Milwaukee. And we just gorged ourselves!! It all was so good. It got to be a Saturday morning treat until it closed...darn!!"

Yes, the Harnisch bakery was a big part of summers in town, but we stayed busy all year long, as you will see....

Fun for all Seasons

"What l missed the most about not living in Presque Isle was the true and distinct four seasons. What I missed the least was the very, very cold winters."

-Tom Finnegan

Living in Presque Isle in the 50's was a special time for me. There always seemed to be something to do, no matter what the time of year. Let's take a trip through the calendar and highlight some great holiday and seasonal memories.

We will begin our tour in February, and of course, that means Valentine's Day. In school we all shared small, store bought valentines, and we all hoped to get as many as we could. I recall that in third grade I had a crush on a beautiful girl, whom I shall not name because I don't want to embarrass her. On the big day we all passed out our valentines, and I was so excited as I saw her approach my desk, and drop the small white envelope in front of me. Even though I knew that she gave valentines to all the kids in our grade, I still felt special that she gave one to me.

I took that envelope home, and read the card inside at least a dozen times. I kept that valentine under my pillow for months. She never knew that I was infatuated with her, and nothing ever came of it, but I never forgot my first crush.

Of course Easter signaled the arrival of Spring with, hopefully, some melting of the massive snow piles that lined the sides of all the roads, both in and out of town. We looked forward to getting the ten days off from school also. The night before Easter was spent coloring the hard boiled eggs, and anticipating the baskets of candy we would get when we woke up. After Mass on Sunday morning we usually had a big meal of ham, potatoes and all the rest of the Easter fixings. We didn't really travel very far for any of the holidays, since most of the people we wanted to see lived either in Presque Isle, or in one of the nearby towns.

My birthday is in May, and I really never had any big parties. Usually we would have family and a few friends over for cake and ice cream. I got a few presents and we all played outside.

Memorial Day always meant that school was officially over for the year and we had three months of VACATION!!!!! Unfortunately, the holiday itself was usually spoiled by bad weather, which can, and does, occur often in the north woods at that time of the year. Cold, possible snow showers, and windy conditions did not bode well for anyone planning a picnic.

June brought warmer weather, and two more treats, both provided by the same people. As I mentioned in the last chapter, the Harnisch family came up from Milwaukee, opened up the bakery for the summer, and put their wooden raft out in the bay of Little Horsehead Lake, where all of the town kids swam. Every kid in town looked forward to that!

Independence Day was hectic and fun! Some years there was a small parade in Presque Isle, but if there wasn't, we all piled in the car and drove to Marenisco to visit relatives, like the Dean family, and my Uncle Bob Rutherford's family. They always had a parade which featured fire trucks, police cars, graders and dump trucks, along with various logging trucks, one of which was driven by my cousin, Stuart Dean.

A quick side note here about Stuart Dean- of all my relatives he was by far the coolest one. Although others in his family were quite religious, Stuart never really fit that mold. Here is the best way I could describe him, and how I will always remember him- If you recall the movie "Hud" and the character that Paul Newman played, in my mind, that was Stuart Dean. I have shared this analogy with many ladies from the area and, for some reason, when I mention his name, a smile comes across their faces......

But back to Marenisco on the 4th of July...After the parade, everyone gathered outside the town hall for pie eating contests, ice cream, games and, of course, lots of beer for the adults. The day ended with the fireworks at dusk, and then we all headed home, tired, but very happy.

Labor Day meant that summer was over and the next day we would be back at school. The Harnisch's had closed up the bakery, and the raft was pulled out of the water and stored away for the winter. Mom had ordered new school clothes from the J.C. Penny's catalogue, and when the big bundle came, we all got to try on our new duds. As much as I enjoyed the summer vacation, I also looked forward to going back to school then, a feeling that would definitely change when I got to Milwaukee and went to school there.

Fall brought colder temperatures, and it was not that unusual to see a few snowflakes in late September or early October. I remember how much fun I had walking to school on those crisp October mornings, when overnight the thermometer had dropped below freezing. That meant that any water puddles on the gravel roads had a thin sheet of ice on them. I made it a point to break thru every puddle that I could. Of course that meant that, by the time I got to class, my feet were soaking wet, but it was worth it, I guess.

The end of October meant Halloween! Unlike today's Halloween rituals that, understandably, are needed for safety, we always trick-or-treated on October 31st, at night. No parental supervision, and always with a homemade costume. For the boys, it was usually a cowboy, a ghost, or a hobo, and most of the girls went as princesses, or witches. We went to almost every house and business in town and we always got great treats. Bob Hill remembers that he loved to trick-or treat at Hilda "Grandma Mac" McKenzie's house, because she always had huge, tasty sugar cookies, and gave each child a nickel as well. And back then, for a kid, a nickel was a lot!

Thanksgiving was, of course, in the middle of the gun deer season, so there was no traveling involved on our part. Dad and Grandpa hunted as much as they could, and once they got their deer, they usually still went out and helped other hunters fill their tags. We still had a big thanksgiving dinner, with turkey and all the trimmings, then outside to play. When I was old enough to help on the deer drives, I usually went to bed pretty early, since Dad wanted to be up and in the woods before dawn. By now there was almost always snow, so tracking the deer was much easier. But, all too soon our short vacation was over, and we were back in school.

The next month seemed to drag on forever, as we were all anticipating the biggest holiday of them all…

Christmas Tree Hunting

Suddenly Dad stopped in his tracks, and put out his arm to halt me as well. "Look, Chum! There!" he whispered, pointing straight ahead. "I think we found it!"

We loved all the holidays- Halloween, Independence Day, birthday celebrations, and Thanksgiving. But the biggest, best, and the one we looked forward to the most, was Christmas. Christmas in the 50's in Winegar was not only significantly different than Christmas in today's culture, it was (in my opinion) significantly better!

The Christmas season back then was not dictated by the retail industry as it is today. The holiday sales push did not start on Labor Day and continue until Christmas Eve, only to then be followed the day after Christmas by massive advertised sales. It was not about how much you could spend, or how many lights and extravagant decorations you could put up in your yard. An artificial tree that costs $150? Wouldn't happen! In fact, let's start our Winegar Christmas there- with the tree.

We didn't have large Christmas tree lots; we didn't have ANY Christmas tree lots. We didn't need any because the trees were FREE! All you had to do was to go out into the woods about a week before

Christmas, trudge through the deep snow (and Winegar always had deep snow in December), search for that perfect (or near perfect) tree, cut it down, drag it out of the forest, put it on your car, and take it home – Griswold style!.

This particular tale takes place in December, 1955. I am 5 years old, and I am with my dad for my very first Christmas tree hunt. Our search begins in the forest just south of Winegar. Last night's snowfall had added a fresh blanket of white fluff on top of the 12 or so inches of already accumulated snow cover. The bright sunlight and the blue, cloudless sky gives me a feeling of warmth, even though the temperature is hovering around 15 degrees above zero. The woods are silent; as quiet as only winter can make them. No animals or birds disturb the peace and serenity of this stretch of timber. The only sounds are the quiet conversations with dad regarding the merits, or demerits, of each tree vying to become the centerpiece of the Rutherford family Christmas.

Now, I should mention that in a lot of ways, my dad was a perfectionist. He was not interested in just getting any old tree; our tree had to be perfect in every way; color, freshness, shape, and symmetry. There were thousands of evergreens growing in the forests surrounding Winegar, and Dad would not be satisfied until he found the very best one. We had already been tree hunting for over two hours when, to be honest, the thrill of this adventure was rapidly wearing off, especially as I struggled to keep up with my dad who was not having nearly as much difficulty navigating the deep snow as I was. I am quite certain that we had already passed judgement on over 100 potential candidates, from blue spruces to Norway pines, and everything in between.

"What do you think of this one, Chum?" (dad always called me that)

Casting a critical eye at the tree (like I actually knew what I was looking for) I would say something like, "I don't know, Dad, it looks a little skinny to me."

"I think you're right, son. Let's keep looking. I know we will find something better."

Or, "Dad! Look at that one!" I would exclaim, pointing to a tall spruce tree. "It looks great!"

"I don't know. It has some bare spots up there on the left side that would be hard to hide. But remember where you saw this one. If we can't find a better one, we may have to come back for it" he would say, as he headed deeper into the woods, with me trailing somewhat reluctantly behind. The search continued....

Suddenly Dad stopped in his tracks, and put out his arm to halt me as well. "Look, Chum! There!" he whispered, pointing straight ahead. "I think we found it!"

There, in a tiny clearing stood a beautiful balsam fir tree. It was approximately 9 feet tall and had to be 4-5 feet across the lower branches. It tapered to the top in an almost perfect (remember, I said "almost perfect") cone. It was, by far, the best tree we had seen all morning.

"What do you think?" dad asked, as he reverently circled the tree, inspecting it from all sides and angles.

At this point, tired, cold, and somewhat bored with the whole tree hunting process, I would have gladly proclaimed that the Charlie Brown Christmas tree was perfect, but I did have to admit that this was one fantastic tree.

"It's great, Dad! Let's take it!"

"Well, let me just take another look to be sure" Dad said, as he continued his evaluation of what I hoped and prayed would be the "chosen one".

Finally, after 2-3 more circuits of the balsam, dad gave his approval and, using his axe, quickly had the tree horizontal. He took hold of a large branch and began dragging the tree back thru the soft snow, being careful not to break any of the branches or lose too many needles. I followed close behind, pretending to help but, in reality, just trying to keep up with him. Luckily for us, what had seemed to be aimless wandering, was actually a somewhat circular route, which put us fairly close to Dad's car. He hoisted the tree onto the roof, tied it down front and back, and off we went to home, hearth, and most importantly, warmth!

Our arrival home brought us to phase two of the tree preparation. As I mentioned above, the tree was ALMOST perfectly shaped, but almost perfect is still not PERFECT. So, once we had the tree positioned in the tree stand, Dad inspected it from all sides, determined where any bare spots were that he could fix, and went for his saw and drill. Since he had cut off a few branches at the bottom of the tree before he put it in the stand, he now had extras to complete the process of creating the PERFECT TREE! After a few strategically placed holes were drilled, and the branches were cut and trimmed to fit, the seven-foot tall tree was ready at last for the final phase- the decorations.

Today, you can buy an artificial tree in a box, take it home, stand it up, and PRESTO! The lights, and ornaments are already in place. Plug it in, sit back and look at how Walmart just decorated your home. Not so at our house! If you think finding the tree and getting it prepped was a long process, you were right. However, it took just as long to decorate, change, decorate, change, and decorate again. First, all the lights had to be placed just right- not too close to each other, but no dark spaces either. And care was also taken so that no two lights of the same color were next to each other. We usually stood back and watched Mom and Dad perform this task, which always produced much heated debate amongst them. After the tree was properly lit, my sisters and I were allowed to hang the ornaments, which we took great care to place appropriately. (My father worked at the White Pine, MI, Copper Mine, and was able to "procure" a number of pure copper spirals, each about six inches long, which really looked nice on the tree, especially since no one else in town had decorations like that).

Now the tree is up, the lights are lit, the ornaments are in place, and thus came the part of the job that I despised the most- hanging the 1000's of strands of tinsel. Mom and Dad sat back and supervised this part, and it seemed like it took forever to hang each individual strand just right. The tree tinseling probably only took 30-45 minutes, but to me it seemed like a lifetime. (Oh, how many times I wished that I could just throw the whole tangled mass of that shiny, silver hair at the tree and hope it looked OK!) Finally, after the tinsel was in place, Dad got the ladder out, climbed up and placed the brightly lit star on the top of the tree. We all stood back and admired this magnificent holiday display that we, as a family, had created.

As for Christmas itself, I am going to let Janis Felts and Kathleen Reitzloff Newberry give you their perspective on what the holiday celebrations were like for their families.

Kathleen Reitzloff Newberry tells us-

"It wasn't until we moved to Winegar that we had a real family Christmas time. My dad and two sisters got the trees and all the kids made a lot of homemade decorations, with a few store bought ornaments. The tree and the decorations were very pretty. Dad and I did the shopping in Ironwood. The presents were mostly clothes, as we were poor people, and Daddy said we needed the clothes more than we needed toys, but there were a few toys for each of us as well. On Christmas Eve, I would get my siblings together and we would sing Christmas songs and I would read to them from the Bible about the birth of Christ. We kept this tradition for my parents for three years. Then I got married and my siblings didn't carry on with it!! But this will always be a special remembrance to me!!

"I also remember in the winter Al Benson would have a skating rink at his place and the town kids would go out there to play and Mrs. Benson would have goodies and hot chocolate for all. Also, by the school there would be a skating rink too. Fun times!!"

Janis Felts describes the celebration at her house-

"I always awaited Christmas morning with great anticipation. Although we didn't get a lot of presents like children do now, we also didn't expect a lot.

"A lot of time went into making things for the decorations on the tree, and we also eagerly awaited the time to bake cookies! We waited until we could use the cookie cutters and help our Mom, and we usually made quite a mess when we got to frost some of the cookies!

"One thing we did back then, that I don't think kids do now is make paper chains from colored construction paper to string around

the tree. That was the first thing we wanted to do. We wanted to see how long we could make the chains, and it was a lot of fun doing that.

"Another event that we looked forward to was the Christmas program at the school. We all had to learn the lines for the different characters we were playing. A stage was made at one end of the gym, and there were curtains on three sides to conceal what was going on until it was "Time for the Show". Santa Claus always put in an appearance and gave out bags of candy with an orange and an apple inside as well. We also had a two- week vacation until after the New Year! Between Christmas and New Year's, my friends and I would go to each other's homes to see what presents everyone got.

"I remember one Christmas when my sister and I both got skis. Dad hid them (or so he thought) but we spotted them behind the tree. There was a big hill behind our house, on property that then belonged to Maytha Shaddock (this is where the P.I. Pub stands now). The hill is now completely tree covered, but back then we had a great time, trudging to the top and then skiing down. Our boots would fill up with snow, and it wasn't long before we were cold and wet, and came back to the house. I don't think we did that very often!

"There was always a huge Christmas dinner with family and relatives, and we always ate at noon. After the meal the women took care of clearing the table and washing the dishes. The men usually sat and talked, or played cards, while the kids played games like checkers or some card games like "Old Maid" or "Go Fish'. Sometimes we went outside to play in the snow, unless it was too cold. Later in the day we would always got to eat the pumpkin or apple pie, and if we wanted more than one piece, well that was okay too!

"Most of the Christmas shopping was done in Ironwood, MI because, at that time, it was a booming mine area, and had stores like Woolworths, Kresges, and McMillans Dime Stores, or things were ordered out of catalogs from Sears, and Montgomery Ward.

"Before bedtime, if there was a radio program on that we liked, we gathered around the radio and listened. Some of the programs I remember were "The Green Hornet", The Shadow"' and "Inner Sanctum"' which was always very scary. We always wanted the shades drawn, so no one could see us. Then, one Christmas we got a Sylvania TV! We thought this was the best thing that could ever happen to us! My dad was so proud that he was able to get this for our family. Of course, the reception wasn't good, and the picture was "snowy" most of the time, but we didn't seem to care. There was an antenna on the roof that could be turned with a rotor to try and achieve the best reception, and that helped a bit. It was hard to fathom at that time that we could see and hear people on TV. Now we know the technology and everyone takes it all for granted, but at that time it was something special. Almost as special as Christmas itself!"

A Boy and His Toys

...Since I had gotten up a good head of steam coming down the hill, my new bike and I shot out onto Main Street like a rocket...

A boy needs his parents. He needs his family, and his friends. He needs the security of a warm, and loving home. He needs good food in order to grow up healthy, and he needs a good education, to prepare him to make his way in the world. All of these are necessary, but in addition to all of that, a boy needs TOYS!

I watch children today at Christmas and birthdays, and I see how many presents they get at these gatherings. Not only does it take 30-60 minutes for them to open all their bounty, and about 95% of it either needs to be plugged in, charged up, or have batteries (not included) installed.

In Winegar, while we didn't get a mountain of presents for Christmas, we knew that we were going to get something special, and we could hardly wait to see what it was. The same held true for birthdays. You might only get one present from your parents, but you knew it was going to be exceptional. Over the years I did get some very nice presents, including BB guns, a bow and arrow set (just for your future reference- if the little neighbor girl runs home crying and has an arrow suction-cupped to the middle of her forehead, you are probably in a lot of trouble- trust me!), two model planes with gas engines (not the remote control models like today; no, these were controlled by a twenty-foot string that you held while you constantly turned in a circle, until dizzy. I also learned that it is possible to make them nosedive into the gravel driveway, but only once), and various other cool toys. But probably the best present was my first brand new bike.

The first house in Winegar that I remember living in was just two houses down the street from the Red and White store. I can't recall any details about the house, except that it was gray and white, but I do retain one indelible memory. It was while living at that house that I taught myself how to ride a bike.

I was six years old, and somehow had come into possession of a small, red, used two-wheel bicycle. It didn't have any training wheels, and I certainly didn't have a helmet, gloves, kneepads, or a cup (which I admit would have come in handy when riding a boy's bike with a notoriously loose fitting chain). I learn a lot of things by trial and error, and this was no exception. Next to the house, the back yard sloped down ever so slightly, a perfect spot for my training.

I would sit on the bike at the top of the slope, push off, then raise my feet and see how far down the hill I could stay upright. At first it wasn't very far at all, but when I fell over, I would get up, go back to the top and try again. After many attempts, I got better at balancing, and started getting a feel for the bike. Soon I was able to go all the way to the bottom without falling, most of the time. During this entire period, I never touched the pedals; I just worked on balance. Once I had that down, I began pedaling and braking.

Before long I was zipping around that yard and having a ball with my new-found skill.

After we moved into the house next to St. Rita's, my parents surprised me for my eighth birthday by taking me to the Coast-to-Coast store in Wakefield, MI and buying me a brand new green and white bike with 24" wheels. I was in heaven!

When we got home they told me that I could ride on our street and the "back" road (McKenzie Place, both of which were gravel), but I was not allowed to go onto Main St. If they saw that I was able to really ride well, then the following summer, I would be able to ride anywhere with no restrictions.

I spent a lot of time on those gravel roads, and by the end of July, Dad lifted the Main St. restriction. I was so excited as I climbed on that bike, and pedaled down Lake Street. I was going to be riding on the blacktop! No more dirt and gravel for this kid! I could hardly wait for the feel of my tires on the pavement, because I just knew it was going to be so much better than the dirt roads.

Unfortunately, two things conspired to ruin this big moment. The first was my obvious over-exuberance at my newly acquired freedom. This over-exuberance manifested itself the second my front tire hit Main St. I literally froze on the bike- I could not steer; I could not brake. Since I had gotten up a good head of steam coming down the hill, my new bike and I shot out onto Main Street like a rocket. Had there been any cars coming from either direction that day, you would not be reading this book, since I would not have been alive to write it.

The second thing that ruined my inaugural foray onto an actual paved road, was the telephone pole that was next to Gunnar Larson's tavern. As I jetted across the street, still unable to perform any muscle movement at all, the bike angled slightly downhill and, as if by its own will, took dead aim at that telephone pole. Closing at approximately the speed of light, or so it seemed, at the very last second, I was able to wrench the wheel to the right just enough, so that I didn't strike the pole head on, but glanced off it hard enough to throw me and my shiny new bike to a wobbly, and eventual, crash landing.

To make matters worse, my father had been watching me from the top of our street, and he now came running to see if I was OK. I had a few bloody scrapes and scratches, but other than that I was in one piece. He picked up my bike, and we walked slowly back up the hill where I then spent the rest of the summer, relegated once again to riding on the dirt.

As much fun as I had with my bike and other toys, it was also a lot of fun to just pack some gear, grab some food, and spend a quiet, peaceful night in the woods. Most of those nights were just that; quiet and peaceful. However, my first forest adventure certainly was far from quiet, and it definitely wasn't peaceful....

It Was A Dark
and Scary Night...

*"Some national parks have long waiting lists for camping
reservations. When you have to wait a year to sleep next
to a tree, something is wrong."*
-George Carlin

Camping!

Most kids today aren't that much different than kids in the 50's
when it comes to their desires about camping. They want to get away
from the city, into the fresh air, dine al fresco, and sleep in a sleeping
bag, listening to the night sounds of the forest.

However, while their desires may be the same, the camping
methods couldn't be more different. Kids today have basically two
choices- family camping, or Scout camping. Both are fine options,
mind you. The family can hook up to their RV, head to a private
campground, or state forest, park in their reserved spot, connect the
electric, water, and sewer hook-ups, and they are set for the weekend.
Meals are prepared on a propane stove, or grill, and while there is
probably a fire going at night, it is just for s'mores and maybe some

marshmallows. They are completely safe, and their parents are always nearby to keep them that way. As a plus, most campgrounds have a lot of recreational activities; basketball courts, heated swimming pools, playground equipment, and organized arts and crafts.

Scout camping is a little different, in that the kids go in a bigger group, and their parents are not necessarily present, unless they are scout leaders or chaperones. Most times, these camp-outs take place at an official Scout facility, complete with cabins, indoor restrooms, showers, full kitchen facilities, and lots of organized, fun things to do. The adults are charged with the responsibility (as they should be) to keep the campers safe, and make sure they have an enjoyable experience. The meals are prepared for the kids, and even the nightly campfire is completely prepared by the scout leaders. The children gather around the fire, roast marshmallows on steel roasting rods, (heaven forbid they should use a wooden stick and risk getting a splinter) eat their s'mores, sing group songs, then head off to bed in their cozy cabins, about 10pm, where they will be safe from the weather and any wild nocturnal beasts that may roam the woods in the dark of night.

There's nothing wrong with either of these camping methods, since they both, at the very least, let the kids enjoy the great outdoors. I am sure they have a lot of safe, organized, fun. With that being said, it was not the camping that I experienced growing up in Presque Isle…

We had an old canvas, four-person tent that was not only heavy, but usually took about a half hour to set up, (and that's if everything went right, which it seldom did), and it had numerous leaks. We also had sleeping bags, sans pillows, and backpacks to carry our meager, but essential, camping equipment.

My cousin, Pat Finnegan, and I decided that we wanted to go camping one summer night, and we told our parents that we wanted to camp out, by ourselves. Not in the back yard as we had done previously, but actually out in the woods. While my mom was a little skeptical, since I was only nine years old and Pat was only ten, she reluctantly gave her permission. My father, and my uncle, Jack Finnegan, decided to make it a bit more interesting. They each bet us a quarter that we would not stay out all night, in the woods, by ourselves. Full of boyhood bravado, we gladly accepted the challenge and, in our minds, were already planning how we would be spending our winnings.

We decided that we would enter the woods from behind the Knotty Pine Inn, and hike to the southwest shore of Mermaid Lake, about a mile away (interestingly, the spot we picked was near the site where my great-uncle, George Rutherford, had been killed in a shoot-out with moonshiners back in 1926, but we didn't know it at the time). My three-year old collie, Skippy, wanted to go with us, but I made him stay back-a decision I would come to regret later that night, as you will soon find out.

Loaded down with our tent, sleeping bags, backpacks, and our Daisy BB guns (mom adamantly refused to let me take my .22 rifle with me), we followed a faint deer trail through the woods to our campsite. Upon our arrival, we looked for the best place to pitch the tent, and set about searching for enough firewood to keep us going through the night. Working together, we soon had a good supply of dry wood, in various sizes, that would provide ample fire for cooking, and warmth. Clearing a circle for our fire, I made a teepee of kindling wood, and using a few kitchen matches, soon had a nice cooking fire lit. Our food for this outing consisted of the basic camping necessities, mainly, one can of pork-and-beans, ten hot dogs, a bag of potato chips, four candy bars, and four bottles of soda. We didn't bother with buns or condiments, since a hot dog on a stick, roasted over an open fire, is delicious all by itself. (This is still true today!).

With the fire going, we now realized our first mistake- we had forgotten the can opener for the beans. Pat got the brilliant idea of trying to chop off the top of the can with our half-dull hatchet. This idea proved to be not quite so brilliant since, after about twenty chops, he had not only succeeded in hacking numerous holes in the middle of the can, but had also reduced the whole thing into an unusable mess that could not be used for cooking. If we would have had those fancy mess kits that were sold in sporting goods stores today, we could have still cooked the beans, but the best we were able to do was to eat them cold, out of the gashes in the can. This was a good learning experience, as I made a mental note to never be caught out in the woods again without a can opener.

To cook the hot dogs, we each pulled out our trusty jack knifes (every boy age six and over carried a jack knife back then) and cut some nice roasting sticks. Holding the hot dogs over the fire, we cooked them until the skin had started to turn black, since that's when the true outdoor flavor is released. We sat back and enjoyed our first meal, savoring the hot dogs, gobbling a big handful of chips, a few spoonful's of cold beans, and washing it all down with a bottle of Coca-Cola. Ahhh.... Could a boy's life get any better?

As the day was quite warm, we decided that a dip in the lake was just what we needed. Since we were located on a somewhat secluded bay, and there were no other people around, we just stripped off our clothes and jumped into the clear, warm, water. We must have spent about an hour horsing around in the lake and, finally worn out, we made our way back to the shore and got dressed.

We spent the next few hours exploring the area around Mermaid Lake and, at one point, stumbled upon the rusted husks of two old Model T cars. They had probably been abandoned there since the '30's and were both riddled with bullet holes. While these holes were most likely the result of someone's target practice, it wasn't a big leap for us to imagine that they were cars that once contained gangsters who had probably had engaged in a shoot-out with federal agents of the FBI!

Returning to camp, we quickly cooked our evening meal; more hot dogs, chips, and soda that had been kept somewhat cool in the lake water, and took another dip in the lake. By now the shadows were getting long, and nightfall would not be far off. We fed the fire for light, and to keep any animals away (we had seen two does, and a fox on our hike in). Sitting by the glow of the fire, we recited every scary story we had ever heard which, in retrospect, was probably not a good idea, since these stories would come back to haunt us in a few hours.

Finally, with the fire burned down enough so that we felt safe in leaving it unattended, we retired to the tent and our sleeping bags. After the day's activities, it wasn't long before we both drifted off into dreamland.

Pat was the first one to be awakened by the noise outside our tent.

"Billy! Billy! Wake up!" he whispered, shaking me.

"Wh- What?" I replied, still half asleep.

"Listen! I think something is out there!"

Now fully awake, I strained to hear what Pat had heard. The woods were quiet for about a minute, and then we both jumped, as something quite large was heard thrashing about somewhere between us, and the lakeshore.

Pat crawled over to the tent door, and pulled back the flap enough to peek out.

"What do you see? What do you see?" I hissed.

"Shhhhh! I can't see anything!" The fire had gone out, and some inopportune clouds had obscured the moon, making our chances of seeing what was lurking outside the tent, almost nil.

"What do you think it is?" I exclaimed, my voice rising, as panic began to take hold.

Pat grabbed me by the shoulders and gave me a rough shake.

"Quiet!" he ordered. "Just settle down! I'm going to go out and see what it is."

"NO! NO! Stay here! Maybe it will go away!" I cried, clutching his arm.

Pat knew he couldn't leave me alone, so we huddled together in the dark tent, and listened to the menacing crashes outside.

It was at this point we realized that things were worse than we originally thought, as we heard noises coming from two separate sides of our campsite!

"What if it's a couple of bears?" I asked, literally shaking with fear.

"I don't think so. Pat whispered, most likely trying to minimize the danger for my benefit. "If it was bears, they would have already torn this tent apart and killed us...."

"Well, what else could it be? Whatever it is they sure are big!"

"It could just be a couple of big raccoons that smelled those leftover beans."

Pat seemed to have calmed quite a bit in the last few minutes, as he now seemed to have convinced himself that we probably were not about to be the main course in a black bear's midnight meal.

I began to notice that the thrashing and crashing had diminished somewhat, as whatever was out there seemed to be moving away from our camp, and back in the direction of town.

We stayed in the tent, cowering together for what seemed like an hour, until the woods quieted down and became still once again. When we thought it was safe, we crawled very cautiously out of the meager protection of the tent. The clouds had dissipated and the full moon gave us some much needed visibility. Pat grabbed some twigs and we quickly built a bonfire that we hoped would dissuade any other creatures from coming near us for the rest of the night. We dragged our sleeping bags out of the tent, and wrapping them around us, we sat by the fire, trying to be as alert as possible for any unwanted visitors. Finally, I could not keep my eyes open anymore, and fell into a troubled, but exhausted sleep. I am sure Pat did the same, as the next thing we both knew, dawn was breaking, and our fire had burned down once again. This was not a problem, since we had eaten almost all of our food, except for two candy bars and a handful of chips.

Camping, by now, had lost much of its original appeal for both of us, and we quickly set about tearing down the tent and packing up for our trip back to the safety and security of our homes. We decided, however, to first scout the area and see if we could determine what kind of beasts had invaded our camp, and caused us so much fear in the middle of the night.

Strangely enough, we did not find any large animal tracks- no bear, deer, raccoon- nothing. Pat however, made the find of the morning, in the soft ground by the shore of the lake.

"Billy! Come here! I found something!" he called.

I quickly made my way over to him. "Look at that! That is what was out here last night!" he said, laughing.

There, clearly visible in the dirt was the large print- of a boot! The mystery of our night visitors had been solved.

"It was our Dads'." Pat explained. "Remember the bets? They came out here to try and scare us! I bet if we had run out of the tent, they would have grabbed us, and laughed their butts off."

"Yeah, but we didn't!" I practically yelled with pride, quickly forgetting the panic of just a few hours ago, "We didn't run! We stayed out here all night, and we won the bet!"

"Let's go collect!" Pat shouted, as he picked up his gear.

Since both our fathers were hard working men, they probably had been at Gunnar's tavern for a while last night, being as it was Friday, and payday. As it was now just a little after 6am, that meant that they were, in all likelihood, both sound asleep. We were determined to change that, and very soon.

We made the hike back to town, dropped our camping gear in Pat's back yard and made our way into the very quiet Finnegan home. It wasn't quiet for long though, as Pat started hollering at the top of his lungs.

"DAD! DAD! WAKE UP! WAKE UP!" he yelled, as he burst into his parent's bedroom, and shook the sleeping form of my Uncle Jack.

"WAKE UP, DAD!" Jack groggily rolled over, and fixed his youngest son with an extremely stern and somewhat frightening look.

"What! What the hell are you yelling about?" he asked.

"We stayed out all night, and now you owe each of us a quarter! Pay up!" Pat demanded.

"You guys were out there all night? Weren't you scared?" Uncle Jack asked, with what I took to be a knowing grin.

"You know we were." Pat answered, "And you, and Billy's dad were out there too. We know it was you, trying to scare us. We saw your tracks!"

Jack just laughed, and rolled over saying, "Go take your money off the kitchen table. Now let me get back to sleep!"

Rushing out to the kitchen Pat scooped up four quarters off the table. Handing me two of them, he said "We deserve extra, for what they tried to do. Now let's go see your dad!"

We made our way up the road to my house. While the scene there was not as loud and scary as it had been at Pat's, we did collect another quarter each, and let my dad get back to sleep.

We spent the morning planning on how we were going to spend our new found and, well deserved, riches. Thoughts of sodas, comic books, and chocolate malts figured prominently in those plans.

We never did get either of our fathers to admit that it was them that were lurking about our camp that night. When asked, they both vigorously denied being anywhere near there. Uncle Jack even went so far as to claim that he didn't even know where Mermaid Lake was, which made all of their denials even more suspect.

I camped out many times after that, with Pat, and with other boys in town, and we loved sharing the harrowing story of our night at Mermaid Lake with everyone. Of course, in the telling and re-telling of that story, somehow our fear and panic were replaced with bravery and courage. I'm sure that, given enough time, we would have told how we chased the intruders through the woods with sticks, until they gave up and ran off in fear of their lives....

I don't think boys today know what they are missing until they have a camping experience like that....

Northwoods Notables

"The strongest man in the world is he who stands most alone."

-Henrik Ibsen

Art LaHa

The following article first appeared in the book *"The History of Wisconsin Bowhunting"*. Excerpts are reprinted here with the permission of the Wisconsin BowHunters Association and the author, Bill McCrary, and will also appear in an updated version of that book, due for release soon:

If ever there was a bowhunting legend in Wisconsin, it would have to be the well-known and renowned Art LaHa. In his time, he was a celebrated bowhunting personality who achieved success, notoriety, and fame on a local, state, and national level.

All this began when, as a teenager in 1936, LaHa received his first bow. A lumberjack friend of the family made it for him from an iron-wood stave. This sparked his interest and sent him on a journey that was to last his entire lifetime.

Starting in Vilas County with subsistence bowhunting during the depression, he went on in succeeding years to bowhunt in 48 of our 50 states, and all 14 Canadian provinces, along with Greenland and Iceland. His list of big game animals taken with a bow and arrow includes black, brown, grizzly, and polar bear, as well as white-tailed deer, elk, caribou, moose, wolves, wolverine, walrus, mountain goat, and Dell sheep. In total his bow harvests numbered 250 individual specimens, many of which were trophy class animals.

LaHa's prowess with the bow is well-known and recognized on a national level, but relatively few are aware of his contributions to bowhunting in the early days of the sport. He promoted bowhunting on a local level by talking to people on the street and by recruiting new members for a club being formed in his area. He soon met and teamed up with Roy Case, later to be the founder of Wisconsin Bowhunters (WBH), and the two worked tirelessly to get the first bow and arrow seasons installed on a permanent basis. For a number of years this was a work in progress, but Case and LaHa partnered with Otto Wilke, Larry Whiffen Sr., Aldo Leopold, and Fred Bear to accomplish this mission.

With time, tenacity, and commitment, this group eventually prevailed. By the mid-1940's bow hunters had regular seasons and were starting to be accepted within the Wisconsin outdoors sporting community, and by the general public. Case and LaHa began to routinely prove the effectiveness of the bow, and became unofficial public good will ambassadors. Their efforts eventually led to full acceptance of the bow as a game management tool, and the recognition that bowhunting was here to stay. LaHa often shared his experiences with others in articles in *Outdoor Life* and *National Bowhunter* magazines.

Vocationally, LaHa wore many hats during his lifetime. As a youngster he held a number of odd jobs and, while in high school, boxed professionally. He was known to travel as far away as New York to meet opponents. During WWII he joined the US Corps of Engineers to do construction on the Alcan Highway.

Returning to Winchester, WI, he raised a family while running a hunting camp, a grocery store, a wholesale meat business, and later, a very successful combination restaurant, bar, and lodge, serving bowhunters in autumn, and skiers and snowmobilers in the winter. Unfortunately, his Bear Bar & Lodge suffered two devastating fires, the last in 1987, which destroyed many of his bowhunting trophies and mementos of a lifetime outdoors. During these years he also found time to operate a small archery tackle business and then to become involved with, and a major stockholder of, the American Archery Company in Oconto Falls.

This busy lifestyle would have overwhelmed many men, but not Art LaHa. He also found time to be a hunting guide. He had fallen in love with Alaska when he worked on the highway during WWII and vowed to return. He did so, 52 times over the years, first as a hunter and then as a guide. He became such a frequent visitor and well-known guide that the Governor named a lake after him, LaHa Lake. He guided over 1,000 hunters in Alaska and his clients harvested nearly every legal species of game found there.

However, probably his greatest passion was to guide bowhunters in his native Wisconsin. Starting in the 1940's, and continuing through the 1983 season, LaHa hosted and guided thousands of resident and non-resident bowhunters in search of deer and bear. Many a neophyte bowhunter harvested their first deer under his tutelage, and then went on to become a repeat visitor at his hunting lodge. He had a quick wit, and easy smile, and a desire to befriend all. This personality combined with his hunting and guiding skills to make his camp a fun place to be and one of, if not THE best, bowhunting camp/guide services in Wisconsin. He officially retired from guiding bowhunters at the end of the 1983 season, but kept his lodge open to accommodate bowhunters for many years.

Art LaHa passed away in 1994, and in April of 1996 was posthumously inducted into the National Bowhunters Hall of Fame. He remains an undeniable presence in camps thoughout the bowhunting community and is remembered by many. His legacy, impact, and teachings will live on for many years in the hearts and memories of those who trekked the north woods with him, and with those who only know him by reputation and wish they could have.

It was a fitting honor that he was inducted into the Wisconsin Bowhunting Hall of Fame in March, 2016, during the 75th anniversary year of the Wisconsin Bowhunters Association. Had men like LaHa not been involved in bowhunting, and the WBH seventy-five years ago, that association would not be celebrating that significant milestone.

So, to Art LaHa, and to those who were his counterparts back in the day, we offer a tip of the camo cap and a hearty "Thank You."

Ralph "Bottles" Capone

In "*Gangster Holidays*" Tom Hollatz writes;

"In the Northwoods there is a certain euphoria at the mere mention of the name Ralph "Bottles" Capone, especially by those who knew him:

"Greatest human being I ever met..."

"He helped my family out..."

"He had a big heart...always loved to help out...."

Ralph James Capone was born on January 12th, 1894, to Gabriel and Teresa Capone of Naples, Italy. In 1922 he followed his younger brother, Al, to Chicago.

During Prohibition, Ralph sold beer as director of liquor sales for the mob. The FBI said that Ralph operated Waukesha Waters, and also engaged in the wholesale distribution of beer. He was called "Bottles" because he also supplied speakeasies with ginger ale and fizz water for mixed drinks.

Prior to his brother Al's conviction of income tax evasion, Ralph himself was convicted of the same crime, and served time in prison from November 7th, 1931 to February 27th, 1934, when he was let out early for good behavior.

It was in the early 1940's that Ralph and his wife purchased the Rex Hotel, in Mercer, Wisconsin, for $65,000. The tavern part of the hotel was known as Billy's Bar. He also owned the Recap Lodge, at Martha Lake in Mercer. He ran slot machines in these places and other establishments in the area. His alleged partner, Jack "Greasy

Thumb" Guzik, was supposed to be one of the heads of the Chicago gambling syndicate.

For some 40 years, until his death, Ralph and Madeline lived in the Mercer area. They enjoyed the Northwoods and were frequent visitors to Little Bohemia, the rustic lodge made famous by John Dillinger and Baby Face Nelson.

In the wilds of the Northwoods, Ralph enjoyed hunting for grouse and other birds. He also enjoyed trips to Canada for moose. He was an avid golfer, had a passion for baseball, and played gin and pinochle. He frequented Minocqua's Belle Isle, and placed bets via the wire, from there to the tracks. And he helped his neighbors:

Emil Wanatka, Jr: "He wasn't a saint, but he was a good guy. The people here really loved him. If a home burned down, he was always first to start a fundraiser to help out. I'm not kidding. If someone needed a handout, Ralph would help. If you needed a bag of groceries, Ralph would help. He was a member of the Lion's Club, too. People don't understand that. I'll go on record and say he was one of the finest people I have ever met."

Everywhere, it seems, there were glowing reports of Ralph's kindness and generosity. There are tales of his fighting a forest fire, shedding tears after shooting a troublesome bear, and taking people in need into his home.

Ralph James Capone died in November, 1974, after several years of illness. He was 81years old.

Porter Dean
"The Barefoot Guide"

The following information was originally published in the book *"Boulder Junction- The Way We Were: 1960 to 2000"*, and is reprinted with the permission of the Boulder Junction Area Historical Society:

Born in 1907 to Charles James Dean, and Olga Ehlers, Porter Dean grew up in the Boulder Junction- Sayner area, engaging in hunting, trapping, and fishing, as did the other young men in the area, always seeking a way of making a living here in the Northwoods. He married a local girl, but they soon separated and went their own ways.

Porter was drafted into World War II and saw a lot of the world. When the war was over, he returned safely to Boulder Junction. He bought a small piece of land on the Manitowish River just above the bridge on Highway M, built a small house as close to the river as was possible- in the days before all the restrictions! He built a pier, sold minnows, rented out boats and canoes, and resumed his guiding career. Porter was a friendly person and never lacked for friends.

One of these friends was a girl named Blanche Johnson. She realized what a great location Porter's place was, and the two of them started to expand the buildings. Blanche was a good cook and soon had a restaurant going with a dining room where people had an unrestricted view of the river upstream and down. She served a popular Sunday buffet and meals that attracted guests from miles around.

It is unknown exactly what happened between Porter and Blanche, but before long Porter was out of the business and looking for a place to live. He bought a lot across from the Pine Cone, where he built a small house. He continued his successful guiding career. An unconventional man, Porter was apparently more comfortable in bare feet, and thus earned the title of "barefoot guide".

During the winter months he restored wooden guide boats. His yard was full of boats in various stages of repair. He shared his home with several handsome dogs, and many friends who stopped in for visits.

As the years went by, Porter was physically unable to carry on his guiding business and became virtually housebound. Several friends stayed in touch with him. Then, on October 12th 1980, when Chauncey Hunt crossed the street to check on him, Porter had passed away. He is buried in the Sayner cemetery next to his parents.

A larger than life figure was created to honor Barefoot's memory and, as a tribute to the fishing guides of the Northwoods, Russ and Pat Rydin, former residents of Boulder Junction, commissioned chainsaw artist Terry Tessmer, to create a sculpture of Porter.

The artist hauled a huge piece of western cedar to Boulder Junction to work on it. Though he had never known Porter, he studied pictures and old movies of this character. At the end of three weeks he had captured the look of the bare feet, the leather band that Porter wore around his right ankle, the double chin, and the weathered look of a fisherman. The figure took on the personality of the real person.

Porter's likeness stood on Main Street for several years. Many, many pictures were snapped of him, and with him. When the Rydins left Boulder Junction, they gave the sculpture of Porter to the town. The sun, rain, snow, and wind had done considerable damage to the figure. He was returned to the artist for refurbishing and now stands in the Boulder Junction Museum along with pictures of other guides and mementos.

Winegar Reflections

"No matter how long it has been between my trips to Presque Isle, when I arrive there, I always feel like I've come home"

-Bill Rutherford

I don't get to visit Presque Isle as often as I would like. The town is different now, some new businesses, some businesses gone forever. Many of the people I knew as a boy are gone now, but some, like Chet, Bob, and Carl, are still there. When I do visit, if time permits, I like to walk the streets- it doesn't take that long. I remember houses, people, events.

All of my recollections that I have written about here, I remember with such clarity, as if it were only yesterday, instead of well over 50 years ago.

I start at the top of Main Street, where the Presque Isle Grade School once stood. The images come flooding back, being in class, Christmas plays, seeing Smokey the Bear visit and talk to us about how "only we could prevent forest fires". We all knew he was a guy in a Smokey suit, but we listened anyway, and we all promised to be careful with matches. Recess, hot lunches, playing in the gym (I once collided with Shirley Hartmann there and I ended up with a black eye- got teased about that a lot); all those things helped shape me into the person I am today.

....The Red and White store, where Clarence Childers worked, is now a bank. Back then it was where we ran at recess to buy penny candy, and the parking lot was the site of a one day, one ride (I think it was the tilt-a-whirl) carnival that Cleary's Dairy brought through town each spring.

I start down the hill and pass the lot where Gus Swanson used to live. He was a quiet little man, who enjoyed fishing. He kept his bottom-tarred boat down by the swimming dock on Little Horsehead. When I think about him, I am somewhat ashamed because of how us kids teased him, when all he wanted was to be left alone.

....Novak's Hardware...I remember that night in 1958, when Lonnie Novak ran from the store screaming for help because her husband, Steve, was dying. People from all over town rushed to her aid, but there was nothing that could be done....

Walking down Church Street I first pass the house where my cousins, the Finnegan boys, lived. They are both gone now, but oh, the fun times we had....

....Before I reach the end of the street where the Lutheran Church stands, I stop in front of the home of one Mr. Henry Rutherford, my grandfather. I remember how he used to save pennies in a Winston cigarette flip-top box. When it was full, he used to stand on his front steps, and toss the coins into the air. My sisters and I scrambled to pick up as many as we could, since even a penny was something to cherish back then....

....Heading back to Main St, I continue my tour, passing the U.S. Post Office where Mae Prosser lived and handled her duties as Postmaster. And the mailbox out front, where Pat Finnegan and I got in trouble for throwing sticky popsicle wrappers into it....

....I walk past the Last Wilderness Café, where The Lure once stood. I pause for a moment to pay homage to Jack and Marie Long. They had no children of their own, but treated all of us as if we were theirs. Marie as a school teacher; Jack as a baseball coach; both of them persevering through the ups and downs of life, which included not one, but two fires that almost destroyed their beloved business....

....I turn and walk up Lake Street to the end. My house is still there, but the original red brick St. Rita's Church is not, having been replaced by a newer, modern church, which I have yet to enter. Some things are just not the same....

....Back down the hill, I pass the house where the Reitzloff family, and then the Peterson family lived. I see the sunken garden plot where Danny Peterson drove his dad's 1956 Chevy into, during his first behind-the-wheel driving experience.

....The building that was once the Mobil Station is still on the corner, but now it is an apartment building. When Aker Palmer ran the station, he used to come up the hill and get my dad if he needed something welded. Dad was an excellent welder, and Aker would always pay him something small for his help.

....Continuing down Main St, I see the empty lot where the home of William S. Winegar once stood. When I lived in town this building housed the summer bakery, run by the Harnish family. As we discussed earlier, the smell of fresh bakery floated over the town each day, and we all loved it....

....Cy Graham's Hardware was across the street. He died in 1957. The building was later the home of Chet's Sporting Goods where, in 1972, I bought my first snowmobile....

....The Tice family lived next door- Milt and Margaret. She was the cook at our school for awhile. I remember David and Mike, but not the rest of the Tice children.

....At the bottom of the hill, was the Standard Oil station, run by Frank Barta and Nancy Forslund. Dad always used to get mad at Frank for overfilling the tank on his new 1957 Chevy, and letting the gas run down the side of the car. Us kids could always stop in and get air in our bike tires and, if we had a few coins, maybe get a soda or a candy bar....

....Across the road from Barta's, where Headwaters Real Estate is now, was the spot where the Bookmobile used to stop in the summer. It was there that I developed my desire for reading, and that desire remains strong today....

I could continue up the hill east on Hwy. B, where the P.I. Pub is, or head west for a little ways on Hwy. W, down to Frank Jirikowic's house, John McGee's tavern, and across from that, the road to the American Legion Post #480 (of which I am now a proud member). The dirt road there winds around the walleye rearing pond, a road that was, one night, the scene of a wild ride with a true friend, Mr. Bob Hill.

Instead, I walk back up Main St. to where I parked my Jeep. I have one more place to visit....

Two miles west of town lies the Evergreen Cemetery. I never visit Presque Isle without stopping here for a walk, except for the winter months, when it is inaccessible.

In town, I remember buildings, events, and dates, but here is where the real memories lie, with the people. My grandfather, a grandmother that I never knew, aunts and uncles- they are all here together, forever, along with friends, acquaintances, and people I didn't know, but who were part of the fabric of the town's history. I make these visits to pay my respects to all of them.

As I enter the gate, I know my family plot is off to my right, but my attention is drawn to the slight rise of ground to my left. The large headstone says "RUTHERFORD" This is the highest point in the cemetery and the final resting place of my great-uncle, George, whom we met in the story of the Winegar Massacre.

I slowly make my way past the markers of the Shadduck family- Maytha, and, to her right, little Bobbie Lehaie. I pause beside the stone that I brought up to mark my grandpa's grave, and I picture him clearly, always either working, or sitting by his woodstove watching and feeding those squirrels in his yard.

I wander, somewhat aimlessly, stopping here and there to let the memories flow as I see the names on the stones- Ray Sensenbrenner, who gave me all those quarters, Harold Zippro, a big, kind man, Lena Barber- she always had such sweet smelling lilac bushes in her yard.

Johnny Eschenbauch is there- I remember going to school with him, as is Keith Reitzloff, both classmates of my sister, Cindy.

I stop by the stone of Alix Garas, and thank him for his part in catching the killers of my great-uncle, so many years ago. Gundar "Gunnar" Larson- I will always remember him in his favorite spot, sitting on that stool in the corner behind his bar, where he could look out onto Main Street.

Axel Olsson, and now recently, his lovely wife Mary, are side by side. He was a deep sea diver, and together they ran a bar west of the cemetery. I went to school with their son, Rodney, and both he and his brother Holger, are fellow members of the American Legion Post here.

I don't spend a lot of time in the back section of the cemetery, since that is the newer section, and I wouldn't know too many of the people interred there. I visit the grave of Roger Peterson, buried beneath the branches of a tall pine tree near the western edge of the grounds.

Making my way back toward Hwy W, I pass by the stone that marks the passing of Fred and Catherine Wolter, and I nod in reverence to their many contributions to improving life here.

As I get in my Jeep and head back to Milwaukee, and my family, I am struck by the thought that while they say that "you can never go home again", if you always keep your hometown in your heart, you never really leave.....

A Million Thanks!

"I'd like to thank the Academy...."

I owe many thanks to many people who have helped me immensely in bringing this book to life. All of them gave of their time and talents, shared their stories, answered my endless number of questions, and provided me with many ideas that led down the different pathways of Memory Lane.

First, and foremost, I need to thank my lovely wife, Ana Julia, for putting up with me throughout this process. You were my sounding board for story ideas; you held down the fort while I made my numerous trips north, and when I was able to get a laugh out of you from what I wrote, I knew I was on the right track. I love you....

To the incredible team of people from the Presque Isle area, and all over Wisconsin: Chet Dumask, Bob and Eileen Hill, Janis Felts, Wayne and Joan McDonald, Carl and Christine Wolter, Cindy Legler, Mae McGlinn, and Kathleen Reitzloff Newberry. I enjoyed every minute that we spent reminiscing together.

To my friends and relatives in other areas: Doris Hoglund, Jackie Charles, Diane Dean, Steven Finnegan, Dorothea Gerovac,

Janet LaRock, and Clara Perron. Facebook has allowed us to connect with each other and share our experiences, and all of you have helped me so much.

To Liza Tuttle, Mrs. Tom Hollatz, Jack Winegar, and Bill McCrary: Thank you for allowing me to use your written material and photographs. Being able to do that saved many hours and days of research. I hope I have represented your works well.

Thanks to Heather Holmes of the Lakeland Times for helping me with research and for allowing me to reprint the story of the murder of my great uncle, George Rutherford.

Two other people deserve a whole lot of recognition here, and they are Soraida Nichols and Nicole Heeti. They were responsible for the copyediting, proof reading, cover design, and graphic layout of the book. In short- after I wrote it, they are the ones that corrected the mistakes and made it readable. Thank you both so much!

And finally to my publisher, Wasteland Press: Thanks for guiding a first time author through the publishing process. I learned so much from you that I may just want to do this again!

Made in the USA
Middletown, DE
16 August 2019